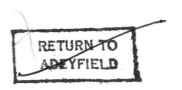

SIR WALTER SCOTT

and his world

SIR WALTER SCOTT

and his world

BY DAVID DAICHES

 THAMES AND HUDSON · LONDON

Printed in Great Britain by Jarrold and Sons Ltd Norwich

ISBN 0 500 13032 9

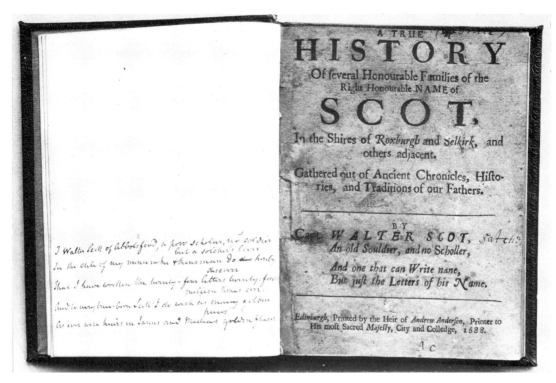

Copy of the *History* by Walter Scot of Satchells presented to Scott by the publisher Constable in 1818

IN APRIL 1808, when Walter Scott was in his thirty-seventh year, and already *Family* known as editor, antiquary and poet, he sat down at Ashestiel, that 'decent farm-house overhanging the Tweed' where he had moved in 1804, to write a fragment of autobiography. He begins by talking of his pedigree, for he was always interested in questions of ancestry and descent, and especially his own:

> My birth was neither distinguished nor sordid. According to the prejudices of my country, it was esteemed *gentle*, as I was connected, though remotely, with ancient families both by my father's and mother's side. My father's grandfather was Walter Scott, well known in Teviotdale by the surname of *Beardie*. He was the second son of Walter Scott, first Laird of Raeburn, who was the third son of Sir William Scott, and the grandson of Walter Scott, commonly called in tradition *Auld Watt*, of Harden. I am therefore lineally descended from that ancient chieftain whose name I have made to ring in many a ditty, and from his fair dame, the Flower of Yarrow – no bad genealogy for a Border minstrel.

Scott links his character as a writer with his ancestry and with the part of Scotland – the Border country, those southern uplands of Scotland that lie adjacent to the

5

Misty autumn morning on the Yarrow

The Eildon Hills, four miles south-east of Abbotsford, the sight of which roused Scott from semi-consciousness on his last journey home

Galashiels, in Scott's day, according to Lockhart, 'the only manufacturing town in his neighbourhood'

English border – where his ancestors had lived and where he had made his home. He defines himself in terms of history and locality, of time and space. These were the dimensions in which, throughout his life, his imagination moved most happily, from the days when as a small boy he absorbed eagerly stories of Border forays and of the Jacobite Rebellion to that final sad journey home from Italy when, disabled in mind and body, he roused himself for almost the last time when he saw his beloved Border hills come into view:

> But as we descended the vale of the Gala he began to gaze about him, and by degrees it was obvious that he was recognizing the features of that familiar land-scape. Presently he murmured a name or two – 'Gala Water, surely – Buckholm

Dryhope Tower, St Mary's Loch

The Eildon Hills from the Tweed Valley

'Beardie', Scott's great-grandfather,
Walter Scott

– Torwoodlee'. As we rounded the hill at Ladhope, and the outline of the
Eildons burst upon him, he became greatly excited, and when turning himself on
the couch his eye caught at length his own towers, at the distance of a mile, he
sprang up with a cry of delight.

So his son-in-law and biographer J. G. Lockhart (who was with him at the time)
describes what was one of Scott's last moments of clear consciousness. It was his
obsession – the word is hardly too strong – with Scottish history and Scottish landscape, always for him most intimately connected, that led his imagination to dwell
on problems of past and present, of continuity and change, of tradition and progress.
For this is the characteristic theme of Scott's finest novels. Place survives, however
altered, while time dissolves; to look at the present site of historic actions, as Scott
loved to do from childhood, is to see simultaneously both what was and what is and
to invite the imagination both to reconstruct the past and to dwell on its relation to
the present.

   Though his home was in the Border country throughout most of his adult life,
Scott was not born there, but at Edinburgh, on 15 August 1771. (There is some
evidence to suggest that Scott was mistaken about the year of his own birth, and
that he was really born on 15 August 1770; but it is far from conclusive, and the
weight of evidence is on the side of the traditional year of 1771.) His father, also
Walter Scott, was born in 1729, eldest son of Robert Scott of Sandy-Knowe and
Barbara Haliburton, who came, in Scott's words, of 'an ancient and respectable
family in Berwickshire'. Robert Scott had gone to sea, but gave up that career after
being shipwrecked near Dundee on his first voyage, and received from his 'chief

9

Walter Scott, Scott's father; and Anne Rutherford, his mother, as an old woman

and relative' Walter Scott of Harden a lease of the farm of Sandy-Knowe, which included the land on which Smailholm Tower is situated. Robert Scott's refusal to go back to sea after his initial misadventure caused a breach with his father, the famous Beardie, with the result that Robert promptly abjured Beardie's Jacobite principles and 'turned Whig on the spot'. This certainly improved his position economically, for Beardie, who had received this name because he had sworn never to shave until the Stuarts were restored to the throne, took up arms in the Jacobite cause in the Rising of 1715, with the result that 'he lost all he had in the world and, as I have heard', his great-grandson continues, 'run a narrow risk of being hanged, had it not been for the interference of Anne, Duchess of Buccleuch and Monmouth.' Scott's father was the first of the family to enter a profession; he was trained as a solicitor and became a Writer to the Signet, a privileged class of Scottish lawyers.

Scott's father was in many respects the model for Mr Fairford in *Redgauntlet*. He was a conscientious, hard-working, not particularly imaginative man, with a moral scrupulousness that prevented him, as his son put it, from making his fortune at the expense of his clients. 'He had zeal for his clients which was almost ludicrous,' Walter recalled in the autobiographical fragment: 'far from coldly discharging the duties of his employment towards them, he thought for them, felt for their honour as for his own, and rather risked disobliging them than neglecting any thing to which he conceived their duty bound him.' He was a Whig and a strict Presbyterian, formal in manner, temperate in habits, whose hobby was Calvinist Church history.

Yet for all his strictness of principles he was, his son assures us, a man of genuine kindness and sweetness of temper. Scott later remembered with distaste 'the discipline of the Presbyterian Sabbath', which he described as 'severely strict'. This is one of the reasons why, as Lockhart tells us, Scott 'took up, early in life, a repugnance to the mode in which public worship is conducted in the Scottish Establishment; and adhered to the sister Church [the Scottish Episcopal Church], whose system of government and discipline he believed to be the fairest copy of the primitive polity, and whose litanies and collects he reverenced as having been transmitted to us from the age immediately succeeding that of the Apostles.' It is clear that it was not only Calvinist strictness but also, and more significantly, a sense of historical continuity that led Scott to abandon his father's Presbyterianism for Scottish Episcopalianism; but his love of continuity was not strong enough to drive him back to his ancestral Roman Catholicism, a form of Christianity which, as his novel *The Abbot* in particular makes abundantly clear, he regarded as corrupted by superstition and fanaticism. But we shall have more to say later about Scott and religion.

Scott's mother was Anne Rutherford, eldest daughter of Dr John Rutherford, Professor of Medicine at Edinburgh University from 1726 to 1765 and a pioneer in the clinical teaching of medicine. She had been educated at a private school in Edinburgh run by Mrs Euphemia ('Effie') Sinclair, all of whose pupils, Scott later told the publisher and antiquary Robert Chambers, 'were, in after life, fond of reading, wrote and spelled admirably, were well acquainted with history and the belles lettres, without neglecting the more homely duties of the needle and accompt book; and perfectly well-bred in society'. From this school Anne Rutherford was sent, with many other of Mrs Sinclair's pupils, to be 'finished off' by the Honourable Mrs Ogilvie, who taught 'a style of manners which would now be considered intolerably stiff'. Chambers adds: 'Such was the effect of this early training upon the mind of Mrs Scott, that even when she approached her eightieth year, she took as much care to avoid touching her chair with her back, as if she had still been under the stern eye of Mrs Ogilvie.'

The Abbot of Unreason.
Scott introduces an Abbot of
Unreason in Chapter IV of
The Abbot

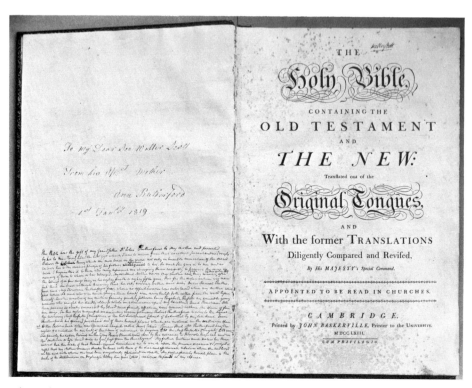

The Baskerville folio Bible given to Scott by his mother on New Year's Day, 1819

Edinburgh   Three years after Scott's birth in Edinburgh, a visiting Englishman, Captain Edward Topham, described the city in a letter to a friend:

> The situation of Edinburgh is probably as extraordinary an one as can well be imagined for a metropolis. The immense hills, on which great part of it is built, tho' they make the views uncommonly magnificent, not only in many places render it impassable for carriages, but very fatiguing for walking. The principal or great street runs along the ridge of a very high hill, which, taking its rise from the palace of Holyrood House, ascends, and not very gradually, for the length of a mile and a quarter, and after opening a spacious area, terminates in the castle.

This 'principal or great street' was the High Street, which ran along the sloping ridge from the Castle to Holyrood, incomparable, in Topham's view, with respect to length or breadth throughout Europe (if only 'they would be at the expence of removing some obstacles which obstruct the view'). The High Street had for centuries defined the city. At right angles to it ran the narrow wynds and closes, parallel to each other, giving the whole an appearance that has been compared to

12

Panoramic view of the city of Edinburgh, 1790

The High Street, Edinburgh, before the removal of the Luckenbooths. Looking west towards
the Lawnmarket

a herring bone and, as well, to 'a turtle, of which the castle is the head, the high street the ridge of the back, the *wynds* and *closes* the shelving sides, and the palace of Holyroodhouse the tail'. These narrow streets, flanked by tall buildings containing flats each occupied by a separate family, were limited in extent on the north side of the High Street, where the ground sloped steeply to the North Loch, a body of water situated where Princes Street Gardens now lie. They tended to be longer on the south side, where the ground sloped more gently, but even so the general impression of the Old Town of Edinburgh was of a group of narrow streets running at right angles into the protective High Street and prevented from further expansion by the lie of the land. This was the old medieval city, surprisingly little changed by the middle of the eighteenth century. To complete the picture we must include the Cowgate, running parallel to the High Street some distance to the south, from which a number of wynds went off at right angles, on both the north and south sides. In one of these, College Wynd, a narrow street rising southwards from the Cowgate towards the old College, Walter Scott was born.

In the Canto IV of *Marmion* Scott described his native city as it appeared to an early sixteenth-century eye, but also as it appeared to him:

> *Such dusky grandeur clothed the height*
> *Where the huge Castle holds its state*
> *And all the steep slope down,*
> *Whose ridgy back heaves to the sky,*
> *Piled deep and massy, close and high,*
> *Mine own romantic town!*

A romantic town indeed, but Edinburgh had paid a price for its romantic air. 'Edinburgh was, at the beginning of George III's reign [the 1760s], a picturesque, odorous, inconvenient, old-fashioned town, of about seventy thousand inhabitants. It had no court, no factories, no commerce; but there was a nest of lawyers in it, attending upon the Court of Session, and a considerable number of Scotch gentry – one of whom then passed as rich with a thousand a year – gave it the benefit of their presence during the winter. Thus the town had lived for some ages, during which political discontent and division had kept the country poor.' So wrote Robert Chambers, looking back in the year after Scott's death on Edinburgh as it had been when Scott was born. There can be no doubt that the Edinburgh of Scott's infancy was crowded, dirty and – in the Old Town at least – insalubrious. It was both picturesque and cosy, but it could be fatal. The young Edinburgh poet Robert Fergusson, soon to die at the age of twenty-four in the Edinburgh public bedlam, wrote of Edinburgh when Scott was not yet five months old:

Auld Reekie! thou'rt a canty hole,
A bield [shelter] for mony a cauldrife [spiritless] soul,
  Wha snugly at thine ingle loll,
    Baith warm and couth;
  While round they gar the bicker roll [make the glass circulate]
    To weet their mouth.

'Auld Reekie', Old Smokey, because the Fife housewives on the other side of the Firth of Forth could tell when it was dinner-time in Edinburgh by the pall of smoke which went up from the crowded chimneys on the High Street and in the wynds and closes. It was a hard-drinking city, too, the professional men drinking lavishly of claret, and those who could not afford it drinking ale, with whisky coming in more and more from the Highlands as the eighteenth century progressed.

It was fortunate for Scott and for literature that Edinburgh was starting to move out of the strait-jacket of the Old Town at the time when he was born. Already in 1752 far-reaching proposals had been made for the expansion of the city. The author of these proposals could find few advantages in Edinburgh except that it was 'the metropolis of Scotland when a separate kingdom, and [still] the chief city of North Britain'. He went on:

College Wynd. 'I was born, as I believe, on the 15th August, 1771, in a house belonging to my father, at the head of the College Wynd. It was pulled down with others to make room for the northern front of the new college.' (Scott)

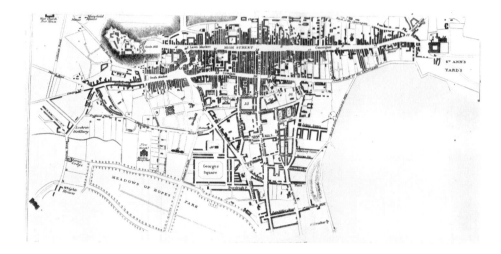

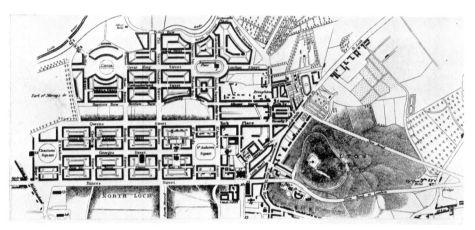

Edinburgh Old Town (*above top*) was served by three main arteries – Lawnmarket, High Street and Canongate – off which ran the wynds and closes. Edinburgh New Town (*above*) had an elegantly regular lay-out

George Square, Edinburgh, designed by the architect James Brown

The healthfulness of its situation, and its neighbourhood to the *Forth*, must no doubt be admitted as very favourable circumstances. But how greatly are these overbalanced by other disadvantages almost without number? Placed upon a ridge of a hill, it admits but of one good street, running from east to west; and even this is tolerably accessible only from one quarter. The narrow lanes leading to the north and south, by reason of their steepness, narrowness, and dirtiness, can only be considered as so many unavoidable nuisances. Confined by the small compass of the walls, and the narrow limits of the royalty [jurisdiction of the city government conferred by royal charter], which scarce extends beyond the walls, the houses stand more crowded than in any other town in *Europe*, and are built to a height that is almost incredible. Hence necessarily follows a great want of free air, light, cleanliness, and every other comfortable accommodation. Hence also many families, sometimes no less than ten or a dozen, are obliged to live overhead of each other in the same building; where, to all the other inconveniences, is added that of a common stair, which is no other in effect than an upright street, constantly dark and dirty.

People were becoming concerned, and the city began to expand beyond the herring bone or tortoise, first to the south, then, more ambitiously and magnificently, after the bridging of the valley to the north, on the other side of the now drained North Loch where the finely planned New Town arose in the latter part of the eighteenth and the early part of the nineteenth centuries. Scott's life spanned the most significant of these developments. In the decade before his birth Brown Square and then George Square were laid out, south of the Cowgate and outside the royalty (though the royalty was later expanded), and the latter became the home of some of the most fashionable and some of the most important inhabitants of Edinburgh, including the Duchess of Gordon, the Countess of Sutherland, Lord Melville, Viscount Duncan, and Lord Braxfield, the original of R. L. Stevenson's Weir of Hermiston. And it was to George Square that Scott's father moved with his family when young Walter was still an infant. The result was that of the first six children born to Anne Rutherford Scott when they lived in the Old Town not one survived infancy, while Walter, breathing the purer air of George Square, 'was an uncommonly healthy child' and 'showed every sign of health and strength' – until at the age of about eighteen months he was stricken with what we now know to have been poliomyelitis, which left him permanently lame in his right leg.

It was young Walter's maternal grandfather, Dr Rutherford, who suggested that country air and exercise might be the best cure for the disabled leg, with the result that he was packed off with a maid to his paternal grandfather's farmhouse of Sandy-Knowe. 'It is here at Sandy-Knowe,' wrote Scott, 'that I have the first consciousness of existence.' Sandy-Knowe (or Sandyknowe as it is now spelled) lies in Tweeddale

Sandy-Knowe

about half-way between Kelso and Melrose, in Border moorland. On the southern horizon, some sixteen miles away, one can see on a reasonably clear day the sweep of the Cheviot Hills. On the other side of the Tweed, to the west, are the Eildon Hills, and behind them Ettrick Water and Ettrick Forest. Something over ten miles away, due west, was the site on which Scott was to build Abbotsford, his pride and folly. Not far to the north-west is Lauderdale, and five miles westward of that flows Gala Water, the sight of which revived Scott's consciousness on his last journey home, with the Moorfoot Hills beyond that. This is the true Scott country, the country of Scott's ancestors, the country which first captured his imagination and held it till it dissolved in death.

They tried some extraordinary treatments on the little boy, but they were all unsuccessful: Scott grew up to be a vigorous and active youngster, but he remained permanently lame, not to any conspicuously deforming degree, though visibly worse in his last years of worry and illness. 'Among the odd remedies recurred to to aid my lameness, some one had recommended that so often as a sheep was killed for the use of the family, I should be stripped, and swathed up in the skin warm as it was flayed from the carcass of the animal. In this Tartar-like habiliment I well remember lying upon the floor of the little parlour in the farmhouse, while my grandfather, a venerable old man with white hair, used every excitement to make me try to crawl.' Robert Scott, the 'venerable old man', died before young Walter reached four years of age, yet his grandson remembered him well. All his life Scott possessed a truly phenomenal memory, of which there is ample evidence, and there is no doubt

(*Far left*) Ettrick Water

Robert Scott of Sandyknowe, Scott's grandfather

that he remembered clearly events that occurred in his fourth year and even earlier. Indeed, his literary art was based on memory: he learned about the recent past by listening eagerly to the memories of survivors of distant adventures, and his most fruitful approach to history was through a chain of recollection.

The little boy at Sandy-Knowe absorbed eagerly every kind of lore and reminiscence. Listening to Jacobite songs and tales imbued in him 'a very strong prejudice in favour of the Stuart family', a prejudice which, he tells us, 'was deeply confirmed by stories told in my hearing of the cruelties exercised in the executions at Carlisle, and in the Highlands, after the battle of Culloden. One or two of our own distant

The Battle of Culloden. The final defeat of the Jacobites was a theme which fascinated Scott all his life. Two of his finest novels, *Waverley* and *Redgauntlet*, deal with the Jacobite Movement

relations had fallen on that occasion, and I remember detesting the name of Cumberland [the Duke of Cumberland, 'Butcher' Cumberland, who commanded King George's troops] with more than infant hatred. Mr Curle, farmer at Yetbyre, husband of one of my aunts, had been present at their execution; and it was probably from him that I first heard these tragic tales which made so great an impression on me.' And he heard stories of Border raids and depredations, in some of which some of his own ancestors had taken part, and his Aunt Janet (Jenny) read him the ballad of *Hardyknute* from Allan Ramsay's *Tea-Table Miscellany* (this is a skilful imitation ballad of forty-four eight-line stanzas written at the beginning of the century by Lady Wardlaw) which he learned by heart, shouting it forth with relish to the great annoyance of a visiting clergyman who exclaimed on one occasion: 'One may as well speak in the mouth of a cannon as where that child is.' In a copy of the *Tea-Table Miscellany* which he later owned Scott wrote: 'This book belonged to my grandfather, Robert Scott, and out of it I was taught Hardiknute by heart before I could read the ballad myself. It was the first poem I ever learnt – the last I shall ever forget.'

Whether or not Scott had gone to live for a while at Sandy-Knowe as a very little boy he would certainly have had the historical imagination that he was to show in his poems and novels, but it is tempting to believe that Sandy-Knowe gave a very special cast to his historical imagination. It certainly occupied a very special place in his memory. In the Introduction to Canto III of *Marmion*, written in 1808 and addressed to his close friend William Erskine, he recalled the family circle there and paid tribute to his grandfather:

> *Still, with vain fondness, could I trace*
> *Anew, each kind familiar face,*
> *That brighten'd at our evening fire!*
> *From the thatch'd mansion's grey-hair'd Sire,*
> *Wise without learning, plain and good,*
> *And sprung of Scotland's gentler blood; ...*

He himself was

> *wayward, bold, and wild,*
> *A self-will'd imp, a grandame's child;*
> *But half a plague, and half a jest,*
> *Was still endured, beloved, caress'd.*

Most important of all in this autobiographical Introduction is his general picture of the influence on him of Border scenery and Border story:

> *Thus while I ape the measure wild*
> *Of tales that charm'd me yet a child,*

20

The manuscript of *Marmion*. At this time ▶
Scott's handwriting was clear and legible

Where hedge-rows spread a verdant screen
And spires and forests intervene
And the neat cottage peeps between?
No, no! for there will he exchange
His dark Lochaber's boundless range
Nor for gay Devon's meads forsake
Benneris grey and Garry's lake.

Thus, while I ape the measure wild
Of ~~tales~~ that charmed me yet a child
Rude though they be still with the ~~harp~~ chime
Returns the thoughts of early ~~harp~~ time
And feelings waked in lifes first day +
Glow in the line and prompt the lay.
Then rise that hill, that mountain tower +
That fixd Attentions dawning hour
Where no broad river swept along
To wake perchance heroic song
Where sighd no groves in summer gale
To prompt of love a softer tale
Where scarce a puny streamlets speed +
Claimd homage from a shepherds reed
                        lonely
It was a ~~naked~~ scene and wild +
Where ~~naked scene as lonely~~ naked rocks were
                                    rudely piled ?
But ever and anon between
Lay velvet tufts of loveliest green
And well the lonely infant knew
Recesses where the woodbine grew +

Rude though they be, still with the chime
Return the thoughts of early time;
And feelings, roused in life's first day,
Glow in the line, and prompt the lay.
Then rise those crags, that mountain tower,
Which charm'd my fancy's wakening hour.
Though no broad river swept along,
To claim, perchance, heroic song;
Though sigh'd no groves in summer gale,
To prompt of love a softer tale;
Though scarce a puny streamlet's speed
Claim'd homage from a shepherd's reed;
Yet was poetic impulse given,
By the green hill and clear blue heaven.

       .   .   .

And still I thought that shatter'd tower [Smailholm Tower]
The mightiest work of human power;
And marvell'd as the aged hind
With some strange tale bewitch'd my mind,
Of forayers, who, with headlong force,
Down from that strength had spurr'd their horse,
Their southern rapine to renew,
Far in the distant cheviot blue,
And, home returning, fill'd the hall
With revel, wassel-rout, and brawl.
Methought that still with trump and clang,
The gateway's broken arches rang;
Methought grim features, seam'd with scars,
Glared through the window's rusty bars,
And ever, by the winter hearth,
Old tales I heard of woe or mirth,
Of lovers' slights, of ladies' charms,
Of witches' spells, of warriors' arms;
Of patriot battles, won of old
By Wallace wight and Bruce the bold;
Of later fields of feud and fight,
When, pouring from their Highland height,
The Scottish clans, in headlong sway,
Had swept the scarlet ranks away.

Smailholm Tower and Sandyknowe Farmhouse

The movement is from topography to history, and from local history to national history and patriotic feeling. Yet Scott, though his greatest novels deal with the recent history of his native Scotland, was never simply a patriotic Scottish novelist. One side of him was totally captivated by the glamour of a violent and heroic past; the other side, belonging less to the wild Borders than to enlightened Edinburgh in its Golden Age, believed in reason, moderation, commercial progress, material comfort, and – yes, money-making on as large a scale as possible. It is when there is a real tension between these two sides of his nature that Scott's greatest insights as a novelist emerge. We will not find this tension in his reminiscences of childhood or, except in glimpses, in his early writings. The story of Scott's maturing as a writer is the story of the little boy, enchanted with the scenes and memories of heroic violence, growing up to see the true meaning, in terms of human achievement and of human suffering, of that heroic violence, and finding a novelist's way of letting the enchantment and the sense of reality work together. After all, it is Rebecca in *Ivanhoe* who has the most convincing word on the code of chivalry:

'Glory?' continued Rebecca; 'alas, is the rusted mail which hangs as a hatchment over the champion's dim and mouldering tomb – is the defaced sculpture of the inscription which the ignorant monk can hardly read to the enquiring pilgrim –

23

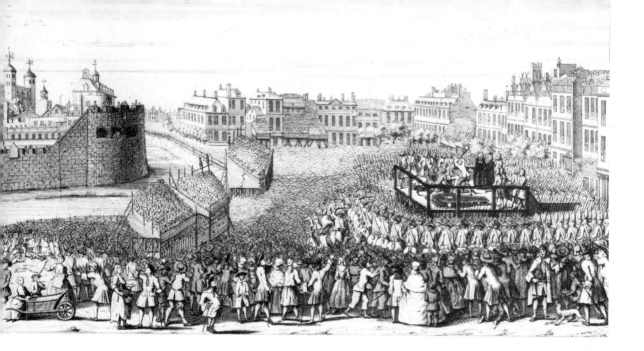

are these sufficient rewards for the sacrifice of every kindly affection, for a life spent miserably that ye may make others miserable? Or is there such virtue in the rude rhymes of a wandering bard, that domestic love, kindly affection, peace and happiness, are so wildly bartered, to become the hero of those ballads which vagabond minstrels sing to drunken churls over their evening ale?'

And the last word on the seductions of Jacobitism is Alick Polwarth's epitaph on the executed Jacobites in *Waverley* –

'The heads are ower the Scotch yate, as they ca' it. It's a great pity of Evan Dhu, who was a very weel-meaning, good-natured man, to be a Hielandman; and indeed so was the Laird o' Glennaquoich too, for that matter, when he wasna in ane o' his tirrivies.' –

and the dismissal of the hapless Redgauntlet, in the novel of that name, as a deluded fanatic who has no part in the modern world.

So while anybody who wants to understand Scott will do well to pay close attention to those early experiences which fed his imagination with 'old unhappy far-off things and battles long ago', he must not stop there. Scott was also, as we shall see, a man of the Enlightenment, someone who was brought in earliest infancy from the picturesque but unhygienic College Wynd to the elegant and salubrious George Square, and who later divided his time between his enormously expensive, gas-illuminated baronial country-house at Abbotsford and a house in the New Town of Edinburgh.

(*Left*) Beheading of the rebel lords on
Tower Hill, 1746

(*Right*) Miniature of Scott aged six,
done at Bath

But it will be a long time before this ambivalence in Scott emerges. His early experiences fed his romantic side exclusively. In his fourth year it was suggested that the waters of Bath might help his lameness, so Aunt Jenny took him there, going first to London by sea. In a brief stay in London the little boy visited Westminster Abbey and the Tower of London and twenty-five years later, on revisiting these places, the grown man was astonished to find out how accurate a memory of them he had retained from that early visit. Scott spent about a year in Bath, where he went to a dame-school and started to learn to read (Aunt Jenny, as one of the domestics at Sandy-Knowe later testified, kept him at his reading 'and by degrees he came to read brawly'). It was at Bath that he saw his first Shakespeare play, *As You Like It*, which made a profound impression on him. All his life he remained devoted to Shakespeare and to the theatre.

After a year in Bath, young Walter returned home to George Square for a short period, then spent some time again at Sandy-Knowe. The following summer (1777) Aunt Jenny took him to Prestonpans on the Firth of Forth to see whether sea-bathing would benefit his lameness. Here he met 'with an old military veteran, Dalgetty by name, who had pitched his tent in that little village, after all his cam-paigns subsisting on an ensign's half-pay, though called by courtesy a Captain. As this old gentleman, who had been in all the German wars, found very few to listen to his tales of military feats, he formed a sort of alliance with me, and I used in-variably to attend him for the pleasure of hearing those communications.'

This character eventually emerges as Captain Dugald Dalgetty in *A Legend of Montrose*. It was also at Prestonpans that he met the original of the Antiquary (in the

Edinburgh from the base of Calton Hill, 1823. Looking up at the Old Town across the North Bridge

novel of that name) in the person of George Constable, a retired lawyer of independent means with an interest in literature and in antiquities. 'He was the first person who told me about Falstaff and Hotspur, and other characters in Shakespeare.'

Early education   From Prestonpans Scott returned to his parents' home in George Square, where he remained until his marriage in 1797. The readjustment from being the indulged only grandson and nephew to being a member of a large family – he had four brothers and a sister – was not easy, and Scott later talked of 'the agony which I internally experienced' in bending his temper to his new circumstances. But he got on particularly well with his mother, who encouraged him in his reading of poetry. He suffered the Presbyterian Sabbath, when reading was restricted to *The Pilgrim's Progress*, a translation of the Swiss poet Salomon Gessner's *Tod Abels* (The Death of Abel) and Elizabeth Rowe's *Letters Moral and Entertaining* (from which Robert Burns had learned his epistolary style): these books did, however, 'relieve the gloom' of the day. His week-day reading was much more varied. He read Pope's Homer aloud to his mother, and she encouraged him to read with expression. He read the songs in Allan Ramsay's *Evergreen*, that pioneer collection of older Scottish poetry, and memorized those that appealed to him most. And in 1779 he was sent to the High School of Edinburgh.

He had already made an impression by his precocity. Mrs Cockburn, author of a modern version of the lament for Flodden, 'The Flowers of the Forest', wrote to a friend after a visit to the Scotts in 1777. She had found young Walter reading *The*

Shipwreck (a poem in three cantos by the eighteenth-century poet William Falconer) to his mother and was impressed by his excitement. 'His passion rose with the storm. He lifted his eyes and hands. "There's the mast gone," says he; "crash it goes! – they will all perish!"' She then discussed Milton with the little prodigy, who expressed his wonder that Adam, newly created by God, should have known everything. 'But when he was told he was created perfect by God, he instantly yielded.' He later told Aunt Jenny that Mrs Cockburn was a virtuoso, like himself. '"Dear Walter," says Aunt Jenny, "what is a virtuoso?" "Don't ye know? Why, it's one who wishes and will know every thing."' Mrs Cockburn described this little six-year-old as 'the most extraordinary genius of a boy I ever saw'.

The High School to which Scott was sent in 1779 was not the present Classical building at the foot of Calton Hill, to which the school migrated in 1828, but a building, then only two years old, situated just south of the eastern end of the Cowgate, which had been built to replace the original school of 1578, the old and distinguished Schola Regia Edinensis. After some brief preliminary attendance at a small private school followed by some private tutoring, the eight-year-old Walter was deemed to have been sufficiently grounded in Latin to join the second class of the High School, taught by Luke Fraser, a good Latinist. After three years with Fraser he moved on to the class of the Rector, Dr Alexander Adam, the most famous of all the rectors of the school and a considerable force in the lively intellectual world of late eighteenth- and early nineteenth-century Edinburgh. He was a distinguished scholar, author of a highly esteemed work, *Roman Antiquities*, and – what was rare in those days – a humane and enthusiastic teacher. Scott's later friend and younger contemporary, Lord Cockburn, who entered the High School eight

The High School that Scott knew

Dr Alexander Adam, Rector of the
High School, Edinburgh

years after him, described Adam thus: 'He was born to teach Latin, some Greek,
and all virtue. In doing so he was generally patient, though not, when intolerably
provoked, without fits of gentle wrath; inspiring to his boys, especially the timid
and backward; enthusiastically delighted with every appearance of talent or good-
ness; a warm encourager by praise, play, and kindness; and constantly under the
strongest sense of duty.' Scott gave similar testimony, declaring how much he owed
Dr Adam and describing his demeanour amid the noise of the classroom thus:
'His "noisy mansion" which to others would have been a melancholy bedlam,
was the pride of his heart; and the only fatigues he felt, amidst din and tumult, and
the necessity of reading themes, hearing lessons, and maintaining some degree of
order at the same time, were relieved by comparing himself to Caesar, who could
dictate to three secretaries at once.'

Scott never became a great Latin scholar, and he never learned Greek. But his
interest in history and in *stories* quickened his Latin studies to the point where he
became able to construe Virgil and Horace and Tacitus and other of the poets
and historians of ancient Rome with speed and facility, if not always with complete
accuracy. Scott had a great gift for learning to *read* a language; he skimped the
grammar, and concentrated on the sense, helped by an almost intuitive feeling for
the meaning of a narrative. He eventually learned to read French, German, Italian
and Spanish in order to read poems (especially narrative poems) and stories, and
he acquired largely by his own exertions a considerable vocabulary in these languages.

It was under Dr Adam's encouragement that Scott, in his own words, 'distinguished [himself] by some attempts at poetical versions from Horace and Virgil':
these include a description of Mount Etna in eruption from the *Aeneid*, III, 571–7,

28

John Graham of Claverhouse, Viscount Dundee. 'Bonnie Dundee' figures prominently in *Old Mortality*

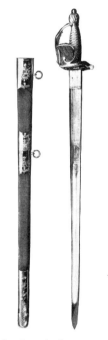

The Sword of Montrose, belonging to Scott

his first known verses, produced in 1782. He was even more active in the horse-play of 'the Yards' (the school playground), being determined to demonstrate, to himself as well as to others, that in spite of his lameness he could fight and climb and manifest physical agility as well as any other boy. He made a name for himself, too, as a story-teller. 'In the winter play hours,' he remembers in his autobiographical fragment, 'when hard exercise was impossible, my tales used to assemble an admiring audience round Lucky Brown's fireside, and happy was he that could sit next to the inexhaustible narrator.'

Young Walter's education at school was assisted by a tutor at home, a young Presbyterian divine called James Mitchell. Mitchell later developed, as Scott put it, 'a very strong turn to fanaticism', and he lived to deplore that so much of the adult Scott's time was devoted to what he called 'the *dulce* rather than the *utile* of composition', but, though the two were totally different in temperament, master and pupil seem to have got on well:

I repeated to him my French lessons, and studied with him my themes in the classics, but not classically. I also acquired, by disputing with him, for this he readily permitted, some knowledge of school-divinity and church-history, and a great acquaintance in particular with the old books describing the early history of the Church of Scotland, the wars and sufferings of the Covenanters, and so forth. I, with a head on fire for chivalry, was a Cavalier; my friend was a Roundhead; I was a Tory, and he was a Whig. I hated Presbyterians, and admired Montrose and his victorious Highlanders; he liked the Presbyterian Ulysses, the dark and politic Argyle; . . . In all these tenets there was no real

29

The Blind Ossian singing and accompanying himself on a harp. 'The tawdry repetitions of the Ossianic phraseology disgusted me rather sooner than might have been expected from my age.' (Scott)

conviction on my part, arising out of acquaintance with the views or principles of either party; nor had my antagonist address enough to turn the debate on such topics. I took up my politics at that period as King Charles II did his religion, from an idea that the Cavalier creed was the more gentlemanlike persuasion of the two.

During his school years Scott read widely on his own, in history, poetry and books of travel. Though his 'tutor thought it almost a sin to open a profane play or poem', he found some volumes of Shakespeare in his mother's dressing-room, 'nor can I easily forget the rapture with which I sate up in my shirt reading them by the light of a fire in her apartment, until the bustle of the family rising from supper warned me it was time to creep back to my bed, where I was supposed to have been safely deposited since nine o'clock.' He became friendly with the blind poet and critic Dr Blacklock, who introduced him to both Ossian and Spenser, both of whom at first delighted him though he soon grew tired of 'the tawdry repetitions of Ossianic phraseology'. Spenser's *Faerie Queene* absolutely enchanted him, and he effortlessly memorized masses of it. His memory rarely seems to have been actively exerted: he just remembered what he liked. 'My memory . . . seldom failed to preserve most tenaciously a favourite passage of poetry, a playhouse ditty, or, above all, a Border-raid ballad; but names, dates, and the other technicalities of history, escaped me in a most melancholy degree.' History he learned at this stage as a series of picturesque anecdotes. 'I gradually assembled much of what was striking and picturesque in historical narrative; and when, in riper years, I attended more to the deduction of general principles, I was furnished with a powerful host of examples in illustration of them.'

30

In his schooldays, too, he read Tasso's *Jerusalem Delivered*, 'through the flat medium of Mr Hoole's translation', and 'above all, I then first became acquainted with Bishop Percy's Reliques of Ancient Poetry'. Percy's *Reliques*, first published in 1765, was the most influential of a number of collections of ballads and early songs and poems which testified to the growing interest in folk-literature and in earlier literature in the latter half of the eighteenth century. It included not only ballads, both genuine, 'improved' and imitated, but also songs (including some Scottish folk-songs) and a variety of Elizabethan and seventeenth-century lyrics. Percy's collection helped to confirm Scott's love of ballads which had been nourished from infancy by oral tradition first encountered at Sandy-Knowe. From early childhood he had been making manuscript collections of poems and ballads of his own. He also began at an early age to form a collection of chapbooks, those rudely printed popular volumes containing anything from old romances to religious tracts which were sold by itinerant pedlars in the countryside. 'My appetite for books was as ample and indiscriminating as it was indefatigable, and I since have had too frequently to repent', he wrote in 1808, 'that few ever read so much, and to so little purpose.' But of course it was this wide reading, coupled with his marvellous memory, that provided the mental furniture required by the future historical novelist. The fullest general account of Scott's private reading in his school and college days will be found in Chapter III of *Waverley*, where the description of the 'sea of books' through which young Edward Waverley 'drove like a vessel without a pilot or a rudder' in his uncle's library is drawn directly from the author's own experience.

Among the books read in childhood that Scott mentions in his autobiographical fragment is the *Histoire des Chevaliers Hospitaliers de S. Jean de Jérusalem appelez*

The Reiver's Wedding, or the *Ballad of Muckle Mou'd Meg*. Scene from an unfinished ballad by Scott on the story of one of his ancestors

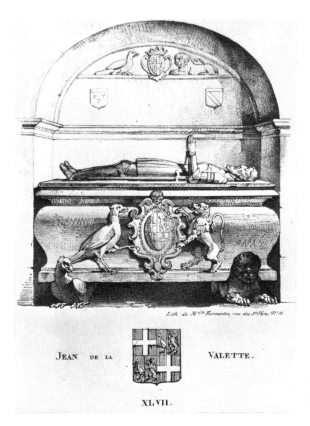

Tomb of Jean de la Valette which Scott visited
in December 1831, when he was in Malta
before proceeding to Italy

depuis les Chevaliers de Rhodes, et aujourd'hui les Chevaliers de Malte, by René Aubert
de Vertot D'Aubeuf, published in 1726. 'I fought my way . . . through Vertot's
Knights of Malta – a book which, as it hovered between history and romance, was
exceedingly dear to me.' In December 1831, with his mind failing after several
strokes, Scott began his last novel, convinced that it was one of his best: the more
coherent parts of it turned out to be almost verbatim reproductions of passages in
Vertot's book, read so long ago. Though he had looked it up again in July 1830, it
was clearly the impact that the book had made in his childhood that preserved it
unconsciously in his memory.

'I left the High School [in 1783] . . . with a great quantity of general information,
ill arranged, indeed, and collected without system, yet deeply impressed upon my
mind; readily assorted by my power of connexion and memory, and gilded, if I
may be permitted to say so, by a vivid and active imagination.' Before proceeding
to Edinburgh University Scott spent some months in the attractive Border town
of Kelso, where his Aunt Jenny now lived, and attended the local grammar school
where his teacher was Mr Lancelot Whale, 'an excellent classical scholar, a
humourist, and a worthy man'. (He had, however, an understandable antipathy

32

to puns, and any allusion to Jonah enraged him.) Under Whale he abandoned the formal study of Latin grammar to develop his facility in reading the language, and considered his time well spent. At this time, too, he read the novels of Samuel Richardson, Henry Fielding and Tobias Smollett, as well as those of Henry Mackenzie, 'the Scottish Man of Feeling', whose novel *The Man of Feeling*, published in the year of Scott's birth, had started a fashion of sentimental writing which Scott was touched by but in which he was never seriously involved. Scott admired Mackenzie, not as a sentimentalist but as a stylist, essayist and novelist of manners, and dedicated his own first novel to him (Mackenzie, born in 1745, lived until 1831).

To his stay in Kelso Scott traced 'distinctly the awaking of that delightful feeling for the beauties of natural objects which has never since deserted me. The neighbour-hood of Kelso, the most beautiful, if not the most romantic village in Scotland, is eminently calculated to awaken these ideas. It presents objects, not only grand in themselves, but venerable from their association.' Here again is the combination of history and topography, of time and place, which so excited Scott's imagination. It is worth quoting a bit more of Scott's own account:

View of Kelso Bridge and Abbey, 1798

Interior of Melrose Abbey, 1798.
Scott regularly took guests and visitors
to the abbey which was just over
three miles from Abbotsford

The meeting of two superb rivers, the Tweed and the Teviot, both renowned in song – the ruins of an ancient Abbey – the more distant vestiges of Roxburgh Castle – the modern mansion of Fleurs, which is so situated as to combine the ideas of ancient baronial grandeur with those of modern taste – are in themselves objects of the first class; yet are so mixed, united, and melted among a thousand other beauties of a less prominent description, that they harmonize into one general picture, and please rather by unison than by concord.

The combination of 'the ideas of ancient baronial grandeur with those of modern taste' was precisely what Scott was to strive for in Abbotsford. But Kelso was to play a more important – indeed, a more fateful – role in Scott's life than to provide examples of natural beauty and nourish ideas of past and present. For sitting next to him at Kelso Grammar School Scott found James Ballantyne, the eldest of three brothers, sons of John Ballantyne, local draper and general merchant. Two of the three, James and John, were to find their lives and fortunes inextricably and in a sense tragically bound up with those of Scott. But during those happy summer days of 1783, young Walter only knew that his new-found schoolfellow James Ballantyne was proving a congenial companion, and the two became good friends.

University   In November 1783 Scott entered Edinburgh University, then generally known as 'the College', its true name still being 'King James's College' (Collegium Jacobi Sexti) ever since James VI of Scotland and I of England had officially granted it this title in 1617, thirty-five years after granting its original charter. The college Scott attended was not the building now known as the 'Old Quad', designed by Robert Adam and modified by William Playfair, for which the foundation-stone was not laid until 1789, but the history-charged and rather run-down old buildings on the same site.

34

James Gordon's *Bird's Eye View of Edinburgh* (after de Wit) ▶
showing the Old University and College Wynd

Twelve may seem a very early age at which to enter university, but it was not unusual in Scotland at that time. David Hume had entered in 1722, before his twelfth birthday, and Henry Mackenzie's name first appears in the Matriculation Album of the University in March 1758, when he was not yet thirteen. University classes were in some respects more like school classes than they are today. The professors orally questioned the students and estimated their progress partly by their answers and partly by general observation. Essays were written for particular classes, but there were no standard written examinations. To gain a degree in the Faculty of Arts, attendance throughout four sessions was required, and the curriculum included Latin, Greek, Rhetoric and Belles Lettres, Logic and Metaphysics. The classes could be taken in any order. But the great majority of students did not in fact qualify for a degree; they simply attended courses in which they were interested or from which they thought they might be most likely to profit. Scott

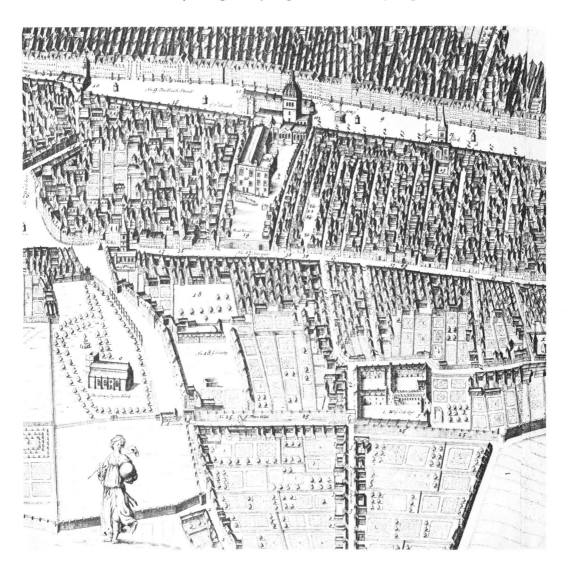

attended the class of John Hill, Professor of Humanity (as Latin was and still is called at Edinburgh University). Hill, Scott tells us in the autobiographical fragment, 'held the reins of discipline very loosely, and though beloved by his students, for he was a good natured man as well as a good scholar, he had not the art of exciting our attention as well as liking. This was a dangerous character with whom to trust one who relished labour as little as I did, and amid the riot of his class I speedily lost much of what I had learned under Adam and Whale.' His attendance at the Greek class of Professor Andrew Dalzell was a dead loss. Unlike many of his fellow students, he had learned no Greek at school, and finding himself hopelessly behind, he stubbornly tried to justify himself by proclaiming his contempt for Greek and his resolution not to learn it – a resolution which he carried out, much to his later regret. He supported his rationalization by a comparison of Homer with Ariosto, greatly to the advantage of the latter, supported, as he himself admitted, 'by a profusion of bad reading and flimsy argument'. The gentle and enthusiastic Dalzell for once lost his temper and pronounced of Scott that dunce he was and dunce he would remain, but at the same time he expressed surprise at the amount of out-of-the-way knowledge that Scott displayed. Later, the two became friends.

In his second year at the University Scott attended the class in Logic and Metaphysics conducted by Professor John Bruce, in which he made sufficiently good progress to be chosen to read an essay before the Principal, the distinguished historian and important figure in the Scottish Enlightenment, William Robertson. But his studies were interrupted, either late in 1785 or early in 1786, by a serious haemorrhage (described by Lockhart as 'the bursting of a blood vessel in the lower bowels'). The illness was long, with several relapses, and the precise dates are in doubt. At first the treatment was drastic. 'I had all the appetite of a growing boy, but was prohibited any sustenance beyond what was absolutely necessary for the support of nature, and that in vegetables alone. Above all, with a considerable disposition to talk, I was not permitted to open my lips without one or two old ladies who watched my couch being ready at once to souse upon me, "imposing silence with a stilly sound". My only refuge was reading and playing at chess.' He read, he tells us, romances, poetry and military history, illustrating the battles he read about 'by the childish expedient of arranging shells, and seeds, and pebbles, so as to represent encountering armies'. He even constructed a model fortress.

Prince Charlie's quaich (a two-eared drinking-cup) owned by Scott

A chart showing all the different
routes of Prince Edward in
Great Britain

Among the books which he acted out in this way was Vertot's *Knights of Malta*, already mentioned as so long remembered.

Scott completed his convalescence in Kelso, where his uncle Captain Robert Scott had retired and bought a villa. Living with his uncle, who was highly sympathetic to his literary interests, Scott found, as he had not found at home, an older member of his family on whom he could regularly depend for encouragement in all his favourite pursuits and whose advice he could seek on his own youthful literary efforts. Before going to Kelso, while still in the early stages of convalescence, he had formally begun his training for the legal profession by entering into a five years' indenture of apprenticeship with his father: for this was the career to which he seemed inevitably destined. In later years he maintained that he would have joined the military profession if it had not been for his lameness. 'My heart is a soldier's,' he wrote to Lady Abercorn in April 1811, 'and always has been though my lameness rendered me unfit for the profession which old as I am I would rather follow than any other.' But he gave up what he called his 'waking dreams' and turned (though not immediately, for he was not yet well enough) to 'the dry and barren wilderness of forms and conveyances'.

A legal profession

37

The drudgery . . . of the office I disliked, and the confinement of the office I detested; but I loved my father, and I felt the rational pride and pleasure of rendering myself useful to him. I was ambitious also; and among my companions in labour the only way to gratify ambition was to labour hard and well. Other circumstances reconciled me in some measure to the confinement. The allowance for copy-money furnished a little fund for the *menus plaisirs* of the circulating library and the Theatre; and this was no trifling incentive to labour. When actually at the oar, no man could pull it harder than I, and I remember writing upwards of 120 folio pages with no interval either for food or rest. Again, the hours of attendance on the office were lightened by the power of choosing my own books and reading them in my own way, which often consisted in beginning at the middle or the end of a volume. . . . My desk usually contained a store of most miscellaneous volumes, especially works of fiction of every kind, which were my supreme delight. I might except novels, unless those of the better or higher class, for though I read many of them, yet it was with more selection than might have been expected.

He was not fond of novels of domestic life, but made an exception for those of Fanny Burney and Henry Mackenzie. 'But all that was adventurous and romantic [he] devoured without much discrimination,' and he 'attempted to imitate what [he] so greatly admired'.

At Edinburgh Scott had the resources of the large circulating library (founded by Allan Ramsay in the 1720s and thought to be the first circulating library in the country) which contained large numbers of the kind of books he especially loved. It was run at this time by James Sibbald, whom Scott described as 'a man of rough manners but of some taste and judgment, [who] cultivated music and poetry . . . in his shop I had a distant view of some literary characters, besides the privilege of ransacking the stores of old French and Italian books, which were in little demand among the bulk of his subscribers'. In the General Preface to the Waverley Novels, which Scott wrote in 1829 as an introduction to a new, annotated 'author's edition' of the novels, he describes this period of his life at some length and gives an account of the circulating library 'which, besides containing a most respectable collection of books of every description, was, as might have been expected, peculiarly rich in works of fiction. It exhibited specimens of every kind, from the romances of chivalry, and the ponderous folios of Cyrus [*Le Grand Cyrus*, by Madeleine de Scudéry, 1648] and Cassandra [*Cassandre*, by Gautier de Costes de La Calprenède, 1642–5], down to the most approved works of later times. I was plunged into this great ocean of reading without compass or pilot.' It was in this library that he first saw, at a distance, Robert Burns, then being lionized by the Edinburgh gentry after the publication of his first volume of poems. These two of

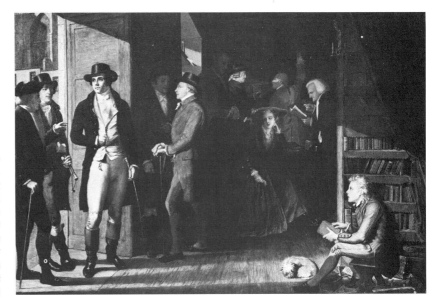

Burns and Scott in James Sibbald's bookshop. 'I fastened . . . like a tiger upon every collection of old songs or romances which chance threw in my way, or which my scrutiny was able to discover on the dusty shelves of James Sibbald's circulating library in the Parliament Square.' (Scott)

the greatest of Scotland's writers actually met only once, in the winter of 1786–7, at the house of Professor Adam Ferguson, the distinguished philosopher. Burns was twenty-eight, and Scott a boy of fifteen, sitting silent in the background while his elders conversed with the famous poet. Burns was struck by some lines of verse inscribed under a picture of a dead soldier being mourned by his widow and child. Scott later recalled the scene for Lockhart. Burns 'asked whose the lines were, and it chanced that nobody but myself remembered that they occur in a half-forgotten poem of Langhorne's, called by the unpromising title of "The Justice of the Peace". I whispered my information to a friend present, who mentioned it to Burns, who rewarded me with a look and a word, which, though of mere civility, I then received with very great pleasure.'

Scott's father, in apprenticing him to himself, left open the possibility of his being called to the Bar rather than practising as a solicitor. Whichever branch of the law he would choose to follow, preliminary training in a solicitor's office was deemed both useful and desirable. And it must not be thought that entry into the legal profession was regarded as in any way stultifying for a potential man of letters. The law occupied a very special place in Edinburgh in the eighteenth and early nineteenth centuries, and men of law were among the leading Scottish men of letters. By the Treaty of Union of 1707 Scotland had joined with England in an 'incorporating union' to become Great Britain, with a single British parliament meeting in Westminster. The Scottish Parliament disappeared, and more and more people came to regard Scotland as 'North Britain' rather than as a separate country with its own culture and traditions. But the Treaty of Union provided that Scotland should keep – as it still does – its own Established Church and its own legal

Glen of the Trossachs

system. The Church and the Law therefore became, in a sense, the custodians of Scottish national identity after 1707 and the law was particularly conscious of this role. Edinburgh, which housed the Court of Session, was a city socially and intellectually dominated by the law. We can quote Edward Topham again, writing about Edinburgh in 1775:

The Gentlemen who are styled Advocates [the Scottish equivalent of the English barrister] in this country, are almost innumerable; for every man who has nothing to do, and no better name to give himself, is called Advocate. Of those, however, who practise and get business, the number is extremely few; but amongst these few, are some men whose abilities are not only an honour to the country itself: Men who make the bar a school of eloquence, and not, as I am sorry to say with us, a jargon of barbarous, and almost unintelligible words, and who preserve, in their debates, the manners and sentiments of a Gentleman.

Many of the so-called *literati*, those historians, philosophers, literary critics and essayists who helped to make the latter part of the eighteenth-century Edinburgh's Golden Age, were trained in the law; some of them were actually judges of the Court of Session. For example, Sir David Dalrymple, who became Lord of Session as Lord Hailes in 1766, was also a distinguished historian, antiquary, editor, essayist, and general man of letters; Henry Home, who became a Lord of Session as Lord Kames in 1752, was a philosopher and literary critic whose *Elements of Criticism* is an important book in the history of criticism; James Burnett, who became Lord of Session in 1767 as Lord Monboddo, produced in his two six-volume works *The Origin and Progress of Language* and *Ancient Metaphysics, or the Science of Universals*, original if sometimes eccentric ideas of which recent intellectual historians are increasingly respectful. Men of law were, in fact, leaders of Edinburgh intellectual life, and study of the law was regarded as a liberal education. Scott knew this, and accepted it. Though he could call himself, in a letter to Anna Seward in 1808, a 'rattle-sculled half-lawyer, half-sportsman, through whose head a regiment of horse has been exercising since he was five years old', the self-depreciation here was not an attack on the legal half. Indeed, he was as a novelist to lean even more heavily and with even more significant results on his legal than on his military knowledge, and his success in rendering in fiction the deeper currents of Scottish history in the generations immediately preceding his own owed much to his sensitive awareness of the fact that lawyers had in Scotland now taken over the functions that used to be performed by men-at-arms. (That is one of the underlying points, with profound tragi-comic implications, of one of his finest novels, *Redgauntlet*, which is full of law and lawyers.) He was also aware that the history of Scots law embodied much of the social history of Scotland, and he used his knowledge of it as a means of illuminating changes in Scottish customs, attitudes and ways of life.

Scott's legal training was not confined to the office. His father had clients in the Borders and in the Perthshire Highlands and Walter was occasionally sent on trips connected with their affairs. In his Introduction to *Rob Roy* he describes such a visit to the Rob Roy country in connection with debts due by Stewart of Appin and the affairs of the MacLarens. A summons had to be executed, and even in the late 1780s 'the king's writ did not pass quite current in the Braes of Balquidder'. 'An escort of a sergeant and six men was obtained from a Highland regiment lying in Stirling; and the author, then a writer's apprentice, equivalent to the honourable situation of an attorney's clerk, was invested with the superintendence of the expedition, with directions to see that the messenger discharged his duty fully, and that the gallant sergeant did not exceed his part by committing violence or plunder. And thus it happened, oddly enough, that the author first entered the romantic scenery of Loch Katrine, of which he may perhaps say he has somewhat extended the reputation, riding in all the dignity of danger, with a front and rear guard, and loaded arms.' Not only did Scott visit scenes associated with the Jacobite Rebellion of 1745 and with other dramatic moments and picturesque characters in Scottish history, he listened avidly to stories of survivors of that earlier and more violent Scotland. It is remarkable how often, in his notes and introductions to those of the Waverley Novels that deal with Scottish history of the immediately preceding century (and they include all his greatest novels), Scott regales the reader with the original anecdotes which he had heard, often as a child or a young man, from someone with a personal or family connection with the events of the time. Scott was constantly picking up this kind of knowledge and storing it in his memory.

The Scottish Enlightenment   It was Scott's friend and former schoolfellow Adam Ferguson, son of Professor Adam Ferguson and later to become (as a result of Scott's influence) Sir Adam Ferguson and Keeper of the Scottish Regalia, who first introduced him to the society of those whom Scott later called 'the most distinguished literati of the old time who still remained, with such young persons as were thought worthy to approach their circle, and listen to their conversation'. This was how he came to be present when Professor Ferguson entertained Burns. These *literati* were leading representatives of an intellectual awakening in eighteenth-century Scotland (especially Edinburgh) which made her philosophers, historians, literary critics, scientists, medical men, portrait-painters and architects famous all over Europe. Some of the greatest of them, such as David Hume the philosopher and historian, who died in 1776, belonged to a generation too early for Scott to have known (but Scott became a close friend of his nephew, also David Hume, who became Professor of Scots Law at Edinburgh, served as a fellow clerk of Session with Scott from 1811, and became a Judge of the Court of Session in 1822). Some, like William Robertson, he knew and admired as a respectful student and reader. A very few, like John Home, author of the play *Douglas*, were friends of the family: Home had been at Bath when the little Walter was staying there and had visited Aunt Jenny there regularly.

These men represented the Scottish Enlightenment, a remarkable development through which Scotland, nationally humiliated and emasculated after abolishing her Parliament and independent national existence in 1707, asserted in a new way her claim to the attention and respect of Europe. The Scottish Enlightenment was in tune with the European movement that combined a belief in reason with a basic optimistic view of human nature. Its spokesmen, though their ordinary speech was very likely to have been a broad Scots, wrote in a carefully studied English, on whose elegance and correctness they prided themselves. But there was also another movement in Scotland in the eighteenth century which arose in direct response to the loss of Scottish nationhood in 1707. This did not express itself in elegant English nor was it concerned with modern 'enlightened' thought. It reasserted

Rob Roy's dirk and purse, owned by Scott

Scotland's nationality by directing attention to its old culture – its great medieval poetry, its ballads and folk-songs, its language, once a great literary language and now (since standard English was the literary language) degenerated into a series of regional dialects. Anthologists of older Scottish poetry, together with revivers, imitators and glorifiers of the once-despised popular folk-songs and ballads, created in certain circles an atmosphere of pride in the national heritage that was of a very different order from the pride felt by the *literati* when they boasted that they could write English better than Englishmen and that their works rather than works by Englishmen now represented British philosophy and historiography on the Continent. The movement had both its creative and its antiquarian aspects. Both were represented early in the century by Allan Ramsay; Robert Fergusson (1750–74), the ill-fated Edinburgh poet, revived a Scots poetic language to produce vivid and colourful pictures of Edinburgh life and, as the climax of this movement, Robert Burns (1759–96) produced a body of poetry in which older Scottish satirical and epistolary forms were given marvellous new expression while Scottish folk-song was re-created in an authentic idiom. Of course, Burns was also much influenced by the Scottish Enlightenment, and could write with great facility in the standard English neo-classic verse idiom of the day. His genteel Edinburgh friends and would-be patrons advised him to concentrate on this side, but fortunately he knew where his real genius lay and for the most part stuck to the kind of poetry he could do best.

It is important to see these two traditions – the international and the national, the genteel and the popular, even, in some respects, the elegant and the coarse – as both working in eighteenth-century Scotland if we are to understand the forces that worked on Scott. For Scott, more than any other writer, was the child of both of them. One might almost say that his head belonged to one and his heart to the other: intellectually, he stood with the Enlightenment, but his imagination had been kindled and his passions aroused by older heroic poetry, ballads, folk-songs, and other legacies of the 'barbaric' past. Similarly, Scott combined a deep Scottish

doubt this is the imperat. 2d. pl. used in its proper sense. There are innumerable instances of the same kind, as *heris*, hear ye, Virg. iii. 27.

GIFF-GAFF, *s.* Mutual giving; mutual obligation; an alliterative term still very common, S.

"*Giff gaff* makes good fellowship." S. Prov. Kelly, p. 114.; more commonly, "*giff-gaff* maks gude friends."

The term seems composed of the pres. and pret. of *gif*, or A.S. *gif-an*, *gif* and *gaf*, q. I give, he gave.

GYIS, GYSS, *s.* 1. "A mask, or masquerade;" Lord Hailes.

He bad gallands ga graith a *gyis*,
And cast up gamountis in the skyis,
The last came out of France.
—Heilie Harlottis in hawtane wyis.
Come in with mony sindrie *gyis*,
Bot yet luche nevir Mahoune.
    Dunbar, Bannatyne Poems, p. 27.

2. A dance after some particular mode or fashion. It is so used by Henrysone as to admit of this signification.

Then came a trip of myce out of thair nest,
Richt tait and trig, all dansand in a *gyss*,
And owre the lyon lansit twyss or thryss.
    Evergreen, i. 189. st. 13.

According to the latter signification, the term is merely Teut. *ghyse*, Fr. *guise*, a mode, a fashion. As used in the former, it is from the same origin with *Gyzard*, q. v.

GYKAT, Maitland Poems, p. 40. V. GILLOT.

GIL, (*g* hard) *s.* A hole, a cavern; *gill*, A. Bor.

—He—drew me doun derne in delf by ane dyke;
Had me hard by the hand quhare ane hurd lay;——
I gryppit graithlie the *gil*,
And every modywart hil;
Bot I mycht pike thare my fyl,
Or penny come out.
    Doug. Virgil, 239. b. 18.

It seems to be used in the West of S. for a kind of small glen or defile.

"This gallant hero, it is well known, had several places of retirement towards the head of this parish, and in the neighbourhood, some of which retain his name to this day; Wallace hill in particular, an eminence near the Galla-law; and a place called Wallace *Gill*, in the Parish of Loudoun, a hollow glen, to which he probably retired for shelter when pursued by his enemies." P. Galston, Ayrs. Statist. Acc. ii. 74.

Rudd. properly refers to Isl. *gil*, hiatus montium, fissura montis. *Geil* also denotes a fissure of any kind. *Geil*, interstitium inter duo praerupta, Gl. Orkneyinga S.

GILD, *s.* Clamour, noise, uproar.

The *gild* and riot Tyrrianis doublit for ioy;
Syne the reird followit of the younkeris of Troy.
    Doug. Virgil, 37. 11.

For throw the *gild* and rerd of mensa yeld,
And egirnes of thare freyndis thaym bcheld,

Schoutand, Row fast; al the woddis resoundis.
    Ibid. 132. 26.

Throw all the land great is the *gild*
Of rustik folk that cry;
Of bleiting sheep, fra they be fild,
Of calves and rowtting ky.
    A. Hume, Chron. S. P. iii. 391.

Isl. *gelld*, clamor, tumultus, from *giol*, vocifero; Dan. *giell-er*, resonare; Teut. *ghill-en*, stridere; Heb. גיל, *gool*, exultavit, tripudiavit. *Yell*, E. has the same source. Only we have retained the *g*, as also in *Gowl*, and *Gale*, q. v.

GILD, *adj.* Loud. "*A gild laughter*, i. e. loud;" Rudd., S. B.

From the same origin with the *s.*

GILD, *adj.* 1. Strong, well-grown.

"Ane *gild* oxe is apprised [in Orkney] to 15. meales, and ane wedder is four meales." Skene, Verb. Sign. vo. *Serplaith.*

This is a Su.G. phrase. Ihre informs us, that *en gild oxe* is one that is full-grown. A person come to maturity, especially if robust, is called *en gild man*; *gild*, *gill*, validus, robustus. The same writer observes, that the former phrase is used in the same sense in Belg.

2. Great. "*A gild rogue*, a great wag or rogue;" Rudd., S. B.

GILD, GILDE, *s.* A society or fraternity instituted for some particular purpose, S.

We meet with a statute in favour of the Merchant Gild so early as the reign of William the Lion.

"The merchants of the realme sall have their merchant *gilde*: and sall enjoy and posses the samine; with libertie to buy and sell in all places, within the bounds of the liberties of burghis." Stat. K. W. c. 35.

For guarding the honour of this fraternity, a Law was made in the Burroughs, perhaps in a later period.

"Na Sowter, Litster, nor Flesher, may be brether of the merchand *gilde*; except they sweare that they sall not vse their offices with thair awin hand, bot onlie be servants ynder them. Burrow Lawes, c. 99.

Besides the merchants *gild*, there were other societies to which the same name was given. These were abolished in Berwick, by an act of the merchant *gild*, A. 1283.

"That all particular *gildes* and societies halden & keiped within our burgh hitherto sall be discharged and abrogat. And that all cattell (or *moveable gudes*) awand to them, be law and reason, sall be exhibit, and perteine to this *gild*." Stat. Gild, c. 1. § 2.

Societies known by this designation, were formed, in various countries of Europe, not only for the purpose of trade, but of friendship, of mutual defence, and even of religion.

A.S. *gild*, which primarily signifies tributum, solutio, from *gild-an*, solvere, was secondarily used in the sense of fraternitas, sodalitium; *ceapmannegild*, the merchant's gild. The name, as applied to such societies, had its origin, not only from the con-

3 Q 2

[manuscript marginal note by Scott:] gill for a narrow ravine is often used in the old poem of Flodden field. Watson's text. p. 85. Gilsland in Cumberland is calvnized de Vallibus. From that Barony the family of De Vaux took their name.

Page from Jamieson's *Etymological Dictionary of the Scottish Language*, with manuscript note by Scott relative to a matter he uses in *Marmion*

patriotism that bitterly resented any attempt to abolish specifically Scottish traditions and customs, with a warm welcome for the Union of 1707 and the possibilities of peaceful commercial progress which it held out. The question that lies at the heart of all of Scott's more impressive novels – how can one combine tradition and progress, what is the viability of the old chivalric way of life or of the defeated Jacobite movement in terms of modern civilization? – is what first inspired him to novel-writing. 'It naturally occurred to me,' he wrote in the General Preface to the Waverley Novels, 'that the ancient traditions and high spirit of a people, who living in a civilized age and country, retained so strong a tincture of manners belonging to an early period of society, must afford a subject, favourable for romance, if it should not prove a curious tale marred in the telling.' And the sub-title of *Waverley*, his first novel, which he began in 1805, is ''Tis Sixty Years Since' – sixty from 1805 projects us back to the year of the Jacobite Rebellion of 1745, distant enough to be history yet near enough Scott's own time for him to have talked to those who took part in it.

Scott was now making friends among the young hopefuls of Edinburgh. He had had up till now one special friend, John Irving, with whom he had gone romantic walks and who had visited him regularly in his illness, but now he greatly increased the circle. The closest of his new friends was William Clerk, whose father Sir John Clerk lived in Pennycuik House, which he used to visit and where he enjoyed 'the fine pictures, the beauty of the place, and the flattering hospitality of the owners'. William Clerk and Scott were founder-members of a convivial group known as 'The Club'. At the Club's meetings as at other convivial occasions Scott could down his liquor as boldly as the next man, and we know that on at least one of these occasions, which Lockhart called 'the many merry suppers of this time', he drank too much and made a fool of himself.

Scott's friends at this time included future judges, professors, landed gentlemen and high Government officials. Throughout the rest of his life Scott moved with ease among some of the most important and influential people in Scotland. Later he developed a warm relationship with the Dukes of Buccleuch (his lifetime spanned three of them), with whom he was on terms of respectful intimacy, for he regarded the Duke of Buccleuch as his 'chief', the head of the Scott clan. Scott was not a snob, but he believed in rank and in the importance and public responsibility of the landowning class. But the ambiguities of Scott's social and political views will emerge later.

'It is well known,' wrote Scott in his autobiographical fragment, 'that in Edinburgh one great spur to emulation among youthful students is in those associations called *literary societies*, formed not only for the purpose of debate, but of composition.' Though not a particularly good speaker, he could talk with animation and even brilliance on a subject that had engaged his fancy, and his vast miscellaneous store of knowledge gathered from his wide and undisciplined reading enabled him on occasion to impress his friends as a promising young man of letters.

Scott was back at the University for the 1789–90 session. He attended the moral philosophy class of the famous Professor Dugald Stewart, of whom Lord Cockburn (who attended the class some years later) wrote: 'To me Stewart's lectures were like the opening of the heavens. I felt that I had a soul. His noble views, unfolded in glorious sentences, elevated me into a higher world. . . . Stewart's views changed my whole nature. In short, Dugald Stewart was one of the greatest of didactic orators.' Scott too preferred Stewart's generalized rhetorical presentation of ethical questions to more rigorously technical discussion. Years later he was very active in helping John Wilson ('Christopher North') to the appointment to this same Chair: Wilson was a facile and totally unoriginal thinker who got the substance of all his lectures regularly by post from a friend in London, but he acted out his lectures with such rhetorical gusto and dramatic fervour that he made an enormous reputation and they were always crowded. Scott also attended Professor Alexander Tytler's lectures on Universal History, and, in the sessions 1790–1 and 1791–2, more severe professional lectures on Scots Law and Civil Law. He found the latter dull, but the former, given by David Hume, nephew of the philosopher, impressed him enormously and formed the foundation of the substantial knowledge of the subject that is reflected in so many of the Waverley Novels. This was, to his stimulated imagination, living history. 'I copied over his lectures twice with my own hand,' Scott tells us, 'from notes taken in the class, and when I have had occasion to consult them, I can never sufficiently admire the penetration and clearness of conception which were necessary to the arrangement of the fabric of law, formed originally under the strictest influence of feudal principles, and innovated, altered, and broken in upon by the changes of times, of habits, and of manners, until it resembles some ancient castle, partly entire, partly ruinous, partly dilapidated, patched and altered during the succession of ages by a thousand additions and combinations, yet still exhibiting, with the marks of its antiquity, symptoms of the skill and wisdom of its founders, and capable of being analyzed and made the subject of a methodical plan by an architect who can understand the various styles of the different ages in which it was subject to alteration.' Hume, he says, was such an architect, and in his presentation he combined 'the past state of our legal enactments with the present' and traced 'clearly and judiciously the changes which took place, and the causes which led to them'. Changes and their causes: here lay Scott's definition of history in a nutshell.

Scott had by now determined on the Bar as the branch of the legal profession which he would enter. He and his friend William Clerk together passed their 'Bar trials' in 1791 and 1792, the civil law trial on 30 June 1791 and the Scots law trial on 6 July 1792. On 11 July 1792 he and Clerk 'both assumed the gown with all its duties and honours'. Scott was now an advocate, qualified to plead in the Scottish courts. But he was also an apprentice poet who had tried his hand often at verses; a keen amateur antiquary; an indefatigable reader both of poetry and fiction and of documents of all kinds relating to the past, especially the recent past, of his country; a devoted explorer of the Scottish countryside, especially of those parts with specific historical associations; and a young man who rather took it for granted that life would be good to him and that he would get his own way in the things that mattered most to him. Exactly what those things were he did not yet know.

Scott was a member both of the Literary Society and, from 4 January 1791, of the more famous Speculative Society, which still survives: these provided him with both social and intellectual opportunities. He read an essay, 'On the Origin of the Feudal System', at the 'Spec' on 26 November 1789, having previously sent a rough copy to his uncle Captain Robert Scott at Kelso for his opinion. This essay,

Page of Scott's manuscript of ▶
David Hume's lectures on Scots law

as heir or assignee to the original Disponee, the Notary must express
pointedly how he acquired this right, for otherwise there will be an
obvious inconsistency, Sasine being granted to one man upon a pre-
cept in favour of another between whom apparently there is no connection — 4thly The notary ought to specify that his presence was spe-
=cially asked & required, otherwise he is entitled to little garther as a
publick officer: the same should be mentioned with regard to the
Witnesses, tho' that may not be so essential.

Registration of Sasines. By the Acts. 1617. c. 16. — 1681. c. 17 was introduced a Law directing the Registration of every Sasine within 60 days after it is taken
within the particular record appointed for the district where the
subject lies or within the general one at Edinburgh under the
penalty of absolute & total nullity. Burgage Sasines are in like
manner to be recorded by the Town Clerk of each Burgh in a par-
=ticular register to be kept by him for the purpose & they are held
as null if else where recorded — The date of Registration therefore, not
the date of the Sasine being the rule of preference among Infeftments, it
became necessary that there should be some regulation to secure their being
recorded in the order of their presentation. After several ineffectual
expedients, the Court of exact of Sed. 15 July 1692 directed that a Minute to
be kept at each Record office in which the Title & a general description
of each Sasine is entered at the sight of the presenter, with the date
& hour of presentation, this entry is signed by the keeper & the party
presenting the sasine, & the penalty of the former if he neglects to
enter any Sasine is deprivation & damages to the private party — this
expedient was adopted by the H. 1693. c. 14 & compleats the security of
landed property. We may here observe that it is enough to validate a Sasine
if from the minute Book it appears to have been presented within the
60 days altho' the day of the actual Registration be beyond that term.
It was indeed found upon a solemn inquiry into the practice of Record
keepers thro'out Scotland that the attestation of Registration which is put
upon the Back of the Record is always of even date with the presentation in the Minute Book altho' it was in reality recorded at a
latter date. The Minute Book is often used as an Index to the Record
as it directs to the Volume & page of the Record where every particular
Sasine is to be found, & as it shews as well what Sasines have been
presented for recording as those which are actually recorded it af-
fords an additional security to the lieges which could not have
been expected even from the Record itself. The keeper cannot
refuse

Hermitage Castle, Liddesdale

Douglas ring, found by
Scott in Hermitage
Castle

revised and with the new title 'On the Manners and Customs of the Northern
Nations', he read to Professor Dugald Stewart as part of his regular class work for
the academic year 1790–1. On 14 February 1792 he read an essay 'On the
Authenticity of the Poems of Ossian' and, on 11 December 1792, he read a third
essay, 'On the Origin of the Scandinavian Mythology'. Among the topics of the
debates at the Society in which he participated were: 'Ought any permanent
support to be permitted for the poor?' 'Ought there to be an established religion?'
'Was the putting of Charles the First to death justifiable?' 'Is the personal
inviolability of the chief magistrate in a monarchial government capable of
becoming hostile to the liberties of the people?' (Scott opened these last two debates.)

Scott was admitted to the Bar the day before the closing of the session, so he had
a free summer ahead of him, much of which he spent roaming about the Border
country. He spent some time at Rosebank, his Uncle Robert's house in Kelso, and
from there he made expeditions to see Roman remains in Northumberland and
historical scenes in Upper Tyneside. A trip to the Lake District was cut short by
bad weather. In the autumn, his friend Charles Kerr of Abbotrule having introduced him to his relative Robert Shortreed, who had many connections in
Liddesdale, he went with Shortreed as guide on the first of seven annual 'raids' (as
he called them) to that 'wild and inaccessible' Border area. His aim, in Lockhart's
words, was 'to examine the ruins of the famous castle of Hermitage, and to pick up
some of the ancient *riding ballads*, said to be still preserved among the descendants
of the moss-troopers, who had followed the banner of the Douglasses, when lords
of that grim and remote fastness'. These annual 'raids' into Liddesdale, in which

Scott 'explored every rivulet to its source, and every ruined peel [fortified dwelling which took the form of a massive square tower, characteristic of the Borders and eloquent testimony to their long history of violence] from foundation to battlement', significantly enriched Scott's knowledge of Border Ballads, in which he had so long been interested, and provided much of the material he was to use in the work which first made his reputation, *The Minstrelsy of the Scottish Border*.

In November 1792 Scott and his friend William Clerk began to attend regularly at Parliament House, which had once housed the Scottish Parliament and where now advocates perambulated, with or without their clients, discussing or seeking briefs. Scott's father, as a practising solicitor, was able to give him the occasional brief and to get some solicitor friends to do likewise. But this was largely routine stuff and absorbed little of Scott's intellectual energies. He earned a livelier reputa-tion among his legal colleagues for his skill at story-telling. More significantly, he became bitten with the German bug which Henry Mackenzie had been largely responsible for introducing into Scotland. Looking back in later life on the German fever of the late eighteenth century, Mackenzie wrote: 'Probably the German school of poetry, which about that time became familiar to British readers,

Silhouette of Robert Shortreed, Scott's guide in his explorations of Liddesdale

Mist in Liddesdale

John the Little Scot

This Ballad tho in a more corrupted state
is still a favourite among the common people
in Scotland.

John the Scot was as brave a knight
As ever shook a spear
And he is up to fair England
The king's braid banner to bear

And while he was in fair England
Sae fair his hap did prove
That of the king's ae daughter dear
He wan the heart & love.

But word is gane to the English king
And an angry man was he
And he has sworn by salt & bread
They should it dear abye

(*Left*) *John the Little Scot*, manuscript song collected by Scott in Liddesdale *c.* 1795, but rejected for *The Minstrelsy*

(*Below*) Ettrick, the birthplace of James Hogg, 'the Ettrick Shepherd', a genuine rustic bard who was 'discovered' and much helped by Scott

Portrait of Scott by Raeburn, with Hermitage Castle and the mountains of Liddesdale in the
background

and was particularly captivating to the young from the warmth of its sentiment as well as its romantic narratives, gave this [enthusiastic and imaginative] tone to the poetry of England. . . . This stream of sentimental poetry divided itself into two parts; one of which flowed through supernatural regions of fiction; the other ran quite as much out of the ordinary line of life, and traced sentimental distresses or enjoyments among the lowest of the people.' It was thus the sentimental-romantic side of late eighteenth-century German literature that captivated both Mackenzie and Scott. In April 1788 Mackenzie had read an 'Account of the German Theatre' before the Royal Society of Edinburgh (which he had helped to found in 1783) in which he emphasized the 'sentimental and pathetic writing'. This essay, published in the Society's *Transactions*, was read by Scott with excitement. 'In Edinburgh,' Scott wrote reminiscently in 1830, 'where the remarkable coincidence between the German language and the Lowland Scottish, encouraged young men to approach this newly discovered spring of literature, a class was formed of six or seven intimate friends, who proposed to make themselves acquainted with the German language.' Scott was of course one of this group, who in December 1792 joined a German class conducted by a German physician in Edinburgh by the name of Willich.

In his later reminiscence of his German enthusiasm Scott emphasized that the German dramatists disclaimed 'the pedantry of the unities' and 'sought, at the expense of occasional improbabilities and extravagance, to present life on the stage in its scenes of wildest contrast, and in all its boundless variety of character'. He also stressed 'their fictitious narratives, their ballad poetry, and other branches of their literature, which are particularly apt to bear the stamp of the extravagant and the supernatural'. The first fruit of Scott's German studies was his translation, in April 1796, of Gottfried August Bürger's much-admired ballad *Leonore* (in which the heroine is carried off by her dead lover's ghost and married to him at the grave-side). The enthusiasm of his friends persuaded Scott to publish this anonymously together with his next German effort, a rather freer translation of Bürger's *Der Wilde Jäger*. This little anonymous book, *The Chase, and William and Helen*, was thus Scott's first published work. The first published under his own name was likewise a rendering from the German – a translation of Goethe's play *Goetz von Berlichingen* (*Goetz of Berlichingen*, 1799).

All this was 'prentice work, and up to a point it can be said that the German fever seriously misled Scott's genius, or at least fostered only one side of it, leading him to concentrate on wild sentimental stories which offered little nourishment for that disturbing sense of the movement of history, of the relation of present modes of civilization to earlier codes and manners, which he was to demonstrate so effectively in his novels. Further, though he worked with spirit at his German, he never fully mastered the grammar and there remained many gaps in his vocabulary. Anyone

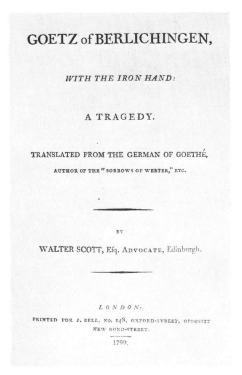

(*Left*) Bürger's *Gedichte*, the copy given to Scott by his aunt and from which he did his first translation from the German. (*Right*) Scott's translation of Goethe's *Goetz von Berlichingen*

who could translate 'Mein Kloster ist Erfurt in Sachsen' as 'My convent is involved in business' obviously had a lot to learn about the German language. Nevertheless, it was his German translations and imitations that started Scott on his literary career. As Sir Herbert Grierson put it, 'it was from German literature that the impulse came which made of the young antiquary and omnivorous reader a creative writer, supplied the spark which fused the love of history and antiquities with the love of poetry and romance.' The fact remains that Scott's greatness as a writer derives from something much more profound than this fusion.

Meanwhile, Scott had been extending his knowledge of Scotland. In the summer of 1793 he spent some time in the Perthshire Highlands with his friend Adam Ferguson, making himself really familiar with the countryside. He stayed with the families of some of his Edinburgh intimates, and from Sir Ralph Abercromby, the grandfather of his friend George Abercromby, at whose country-house of Tullibody he spent some time, he heard first-hand anecdotes of Rob Roy. At another country-house he 'heard another aged gentleman's vivid recollections of all that happened there when John Home, the author of *Douglas*, and other Hanoverian prisoners, escaped from the Highland garrison in 1745'. He made

Exploring Scotland

53

himself intimately acquainted with the scenery of Loch Katrine, an acquaintance he was to put to good use in *The Lady of the Lake*. Scott also visited the passionate military antiquary Patrick Murray of Simprim at his country-seat of Meigle in Forfarshire; from there he visited ruined Dunottar Castle, and it was in the church-yard of the castle, Lockhart tells us, 'that Scott saw for the first and last time Peter Paterson, the living *Old Mortality*. He and Mr Walker,' Lockhart continues, 'the minister of the parish, found the poor man refreshing the epitaphs on the tombs of certain Cameronians who had fallen under the oppression of James the Second's brief insanity.' Scott also visited Glamis, the residence of the Earls of Strathmore, and 'by far the noblest specimen of the real feudal castle that had yet come under his inspection'. (He was later to lament bitterly its subsequent modernization.) It would be fruitless to catalogue all Scott's journeyings during these years. The important point is that he did go on exploring his native country, absorbing local traditions, visiting scenes that are to reappear in his poems and novels, relating particular places to historical events that had occurred there and, most important of all, seeking or encountering by chance old people who could recall the manners and loyalties of former days and had been personally involved either in the Jacobite Rebellion or in some other manifestation of that heroic Scotland whose development from cruel if picturesque violence to peaceful enlightenment and commercial progress Scott could not but welcome while, at the same time, drawn irresistibly to what had passed away. What Robert Shortreed many years later told Lockhart of the significance of the Liddesdale raids to Scott is true of all his Scottish travels during these years: 'He was *makin' himsell* a' the time, but he didna ken maybe what he was about till years had passed. At first he thought o' little, I dare say, but the queerness and the fun.'

Marriage   During these years Scott was nursing a passionate romantic love for Miss Williamina Belsches, daughter of Sir John Stuart-Belsches, a man who was probably not enthusiastic about his daughter's marrying a flighty young advocate of uncertain prospects. Miss Belsches seems to have given Scott some reason to believe that his love was returned, but finally, in October 1796, she married a wealthy young banker and Scott's friends for a while feared for his reason. His pride was hurt, as well as his heart, and he wrote some verses concluding:

> *No longer in my false love's eye*
> *Remained the tear of parting sorrow.*

He got over it, of course, and in fact fell in love again and married just over a year later. But he never forgot his first love, whose memory haunted him all his life. He was thinking of her when he created Green Mantle in *Redgauntlet*, and he refers to her with emotion in the *Journal* he kept in his last years. He fell for Charlotte Carpenter or Charpentier, whom he met when on an expedition to the Lake

54

Glamis Castle which Scott
visited in 1793

District in the late summer of 1797, on the rebound. He pressed his suit with impatience, and they were married at Carlisle on 24 December.

Charlotte, who was born in December 1770, was French, the daughter of Jean-François Charpentier who had been Écuyer du Roi de l'Académie de Lyon. Her mother, who had married a man much her senior, came to London in 1784 or 1785 and Charlotte and her brother were brought up in the Church of England. Mme Charpentier returned to France in 1786 and died there in 1788. The children remained in England under the guardianship of Lord Downshire. There are mysteries about Charlotte's background and about her mother's relationship with Lord Downshire; Lockhart's account of Mme Charpentier as a French Royalist fleeing the Revolution with her children is now known to be an invention.

Scott had to square Lord Downshire before he could marry his ward, and he did so in letters of great tact and courtesy. Charlotte, while no beauty, was gay and vivacious and responded to Scott's own vivacity. She was also worldly and ambitious, in a cheerfully innocent way, and she had firm confidence in Scott's prospects. At this time he was making no more than about £150 a year at the Bar, but he also had an allowance from his father, who was now old and ailing, and who on his death in 1799 left ample provision for his widow and a sum to be divided among each of his children of which Scott's share considerably added to his resources. Charlotte's brother Charles, who through Lord Downshire's influence had got a good job with the East India Company in India (it was then that he had changed the family surname from Charpentier to Carpenter), was also of help, in settling on his sister an annuity of £500.

any idea of the Society in Edin! I am sure the prospect of living there would not horrify you — Your situation would en:
title you to take as great a share in the amusements
of the place as you were disposed to, and when you were tired
of these it should be the study of my life to prevent your
feeling one moments Ennui — When Care comes we will
laugh it away, or if the load is too heavy we will sit
down and share it between us till it ~~to~~ becomes almost as
light as pleasure itself — You are apprehensive of loosing your
liberty but could you but think with how many domestic
pleasures the sacrifice will be repaid you would no longer
think it very frightful — Indisposition may deprive you
of that liberty which you prize so highly & Age
certainly will — O think how much happier
you will find yourself surrounded by
friends who will love you than with
those who will only regard even my
beloved Charlotte while she possesses the power
of interesting or entertaining them — You seem too to doubt
the strength or at least the stability of my Affection — I can
only protest to you most solemnly that a truer never warmd
a Mortals breast and that tho' it may appear suddenly it is not
rashly adopted — You yourself must allow that from the nature
of our acquaintance we are entitled to judge more absolutely
of each other than from a much longer one trammelled with
the usual forms of Life — and tho' I have been ~~or~~
repeatedly in similar situations with amiable & accomplished
women the feelings I entertain for you have ever been strangers
to my bosom except during a period I have often alluded to —
I have settled in my mind to see you on Monday next
I stay thus long to give you time to make what enquiries you

Letter from Scott to Charlotte Carpenter, in which he alludes to his earlier love for Williamina
Belsches

(*Left*) Miniature of Charlotte Carpenter, given to Scott on their engagement. (*Right*) Lady Scott

Twelve years after his marriage, on 21 January 1810, Scott wrote to Lady Abercorn (one of the several titled ladies with whom he long kept up an affectionate and even intimate correspondence) in response to her asking whether he had ever been in love. (The question might be considered impertinent, but the fact that Scott answered it calmly and accurately says something about the nature of this epistolary friendship.) After boasting that he had sold his new narrative poem, *The Lady of the Lake*, for 2,000 guineas, having long ago learned from horse-dealers 'to sell by guineas and buy by pounds', he went on to other matters, including the delicate question that he had been asked, which he answered thus:

Mrs Scott's match and mine was of our own making and proceeded from the most sincere affection on both sides which has rather increased than diminished during twelve years' marriage. But it was something short of love in all its fervour which I suspect people only feel *once* in their lives. Folks who have been nearly drowned in bathing rarely venturing a second time out of their depth.

All the evidence is that he was here speaking the precise truth. Scott came more and more to look on his wife as an affectionate helpmeet, and during the days of their rapidly rising prosperity she was the proud and contented wife of a famous and apparently rich man. When the great financial crash came early in 1826, Charlotte was unable to comprehend or believe the reality, but she was now a sick woman and

57

in fact died some months later. Scott, knowing that she was dying, had gone from Abbotsford to Edinburgh to perform his duties as Clerk of Session (from which he could easily have been excused on such an occasion). He wrote in his *Journal* that 'an adieu might have hurt her; and nothing I could have expressed would have been worth the risk. . . . It withers my heart to think of it, and to recollect that I can hardly hope again to seek confidence and counsel from that ear to which all might be safely confided.' Eleven days after her death he wrote in the *Journal*: 'Alas! I have no companion now with whom I can communicate to relieve the loneliness of these watches of the night.' Later in the *Journal* he mentions how he misses the comfort and attention she gave him and laments that she will never again come into his study when he is working to make up the fire and ask if everything is going all right. Yes; the 'sincere affection' that 'rather increased than diminished' with the years is well attested. Different in temperament though the two partners were, Scott's was a good marriage.

Political views   Meanwhile, the French Revolution had been casting its shadow in Scotland as elsewhere in Europe. At first it had stimulated liberal-minded representatives of the Scottish Enlightenment to hail the dawn of a new and happier age. But as unrest increased, meetings demanding reform proliferated, and (in 1792) a 'Society of the Friends of the People' was founded, accompanied by a widespread expectation among the poor and distressed that radical reforms were imminent, the attitude of the authorities stiffened and revolutionary and even reforming sentiments among gentlemen faded away. Scotland at this time was virtually ruled by Henry Dundas, later Viscount Melville, popularly known as 'King Harry the Ninth'. From 1782 until 1805, in a variety of offices, he ran Scotland on behalf of the administration of Pitt the Younger: there was no pretence at democracy; everything was directly or indirectly in Dundas's hands. This is how Lord Cockburn, who was a Whig and thus spoke from an anti-Government bias, described the situation in Scotland at this time:

A country gentleman with any public principle except devotion to Henry Dundas was viewed as a wonder, or rather as a monster. This was the creed of almost all our merchants, all our removable office-holders, and all our public corporations. . . . With the people suppressed and the Whigs powerless, Government was the master of nearly every individual in Scotland, but especially in Edinburgh, which was the chief seat of influence. The pulpit, the bench, the bar, the colleges, the parliamentary electors, the press, the magistracy, the local institutions, were so completely at the service of the party in power, that the idea of independence, besides being monstrous or absurd, was suppressed by a feeling of conscious ingratitude. Henry Dundas, an Edinburgh man, and well calculated by talent and manner to make despotism popular, was the absolute dictator of

(*Left*) Henry Dundas, first Viscount Melville. (*Right*) Thomas Muir, parliamentary reformer, who was arrested for sedition in 1793

Scotland, and had the means of rewarding submission and of extinguishing opposition beyond what were ever exercised in modern times by one person in any portion of the empire.

Dundas's nephew, Robert Dundas of Arnistoun, had been appointed Lord Advocate in 1789, and uncle and nephew between them stamped out what they considered subversion with ruthless efficiency. The course of the Revolution in France, and the declaration of war between France and Britain in 1793, strengthened their hand, for henceforth those suspected of sympathy with the aims of the French Revolution could be considered traitors and prosecuted for sedition (a crime first brought into Scots law at this time) while executions and terror in France were taken as an awful warning of the dire results that would follow giving in to popular reformist demands. The political trials of 1793 and 1794, at which idealistic reformers were sentenced to transportation, were shameless perversions of justice. 'The great Tory object,' wrote Cockburn, 'was to abuse everybody but themselves, and in particular to ascribe a thirst for bloodshed and anarchy, not merely to their avowed opponents, but to the whole body of the people.' Robert Macqueen, Lord Braxfield, was the most notorious of the bullying judges of this period – 'the Jeffreys of Scotland', Cockburn called him. Braxfield was a neighbour of the Scotts in George Square, and Walter had dedicated to him the Latin thesis (probably written for him by a hack, as the custom then was) he had to present as part of his Bar examinations. He was also on excellent terms with Robert Dundas, whom in a letter of 1819 he called 'my early, kind, and constant friend, who took me up when I was a young fellow of little mark or likelihood'.

Scott, then, was very much on the side of the Establishment in these troubles. Like other gentlemen of the time, and to a greater degree than many, he was throughout his life liable to intermittent panic at the thought of popular insurrections and of mobs in action. 'You are quite right in apprehending a *Jacquerie*; the country is mined below our feet', he wrote to Southey in 1812. In 1819 he was writing to his son Walter, a new-fledged army officer: 'I am sorry to say the people in England seem very unsettled thanks to the mischievous firebrands that mislead them. They have shown however the cloven foot too soon which will alarm everyone who possesses property. I should not be surprised if your first real military experience should be in this most disagreeable duty.' He defended the Massacre of Peterloo of this year, writing hysterically about the prospect of 'an Irish [type of] rebellion with all its horrors' if the magistrates had not called in the military. And he denied that he was taking a party position: 'this seems to involve the great question whether we shall have peace in our time or a bloody and remorseless struggle between property and the populace'. In December 1819 he wrote with melodramatic excitement about the prospect of civil war – 'men go about their ordinary business with musquets in their hands' – and worked himself up into a mood of fear and hatred of the 'populace' which prevented him from even remotely glimpsing the obvious fact that they were fellow Scots suffering under intolerable conditions. He believed the most extraordinary rumours. 'Upwards of 50,000 blackguards are ready to rise between Tyne and Wear,' he wrote to his brother Tom on 23 December 1819. This was nonsense. Cockburn's view was the saner: 'The whole island was suffering from great agricultural and industrial distress. This was taken the usual advantage of by demagogues; and consequently there was considerable political excitement. Its amount in Scotland was contemptible. But it was first exaggerated, and then exhibited as evidence of a revolutionary spirit, . . . It was determined therefore that the folly and violence of our western weavers should be considered as a civil war, and be dealt with accordingly.' But, in the end, there was no civil war, though Scott wrote with great military excitement of preparations to raise volunteers to march all over the place.

All this may make Scott appear a mindless reactionary of the most extreme kind. But in fact his political and social views, which remained very much the same throughout his adult life, were well considered and in some respects perceptive. He feared and hated what the Industrial Revolution was making of workers, and his analysis of the process would have been accepted by Marx. It had destroyed the organic society, in which he profoundly believed. He was a paternalist; he believed in the rights and responsibilities of property; he believed in the dignity of the individual. Two quotations from letters written by Scott in 1820 will make clear his

Walter Scott, second baronet, Scott's elder son. This portrait by Sir William Allan still hangs over the mantelpiece of the library in Abbotsford

position once and for all. He is arguing in favour of arming the poor where they can be trusted, for the great thing is to prevent a class war, 'that most dreadful of evils, a *servile* or Jack Cade sort of war'. He argues thus:

> Several [people have said] the lower classes were not to be trusted. In that case I have replied the 'Game is up' we have only to compute how long the rich can defend themselves against the poor & how long the poor will be of discovering the recondite secret that 100 are stronger than one & so long & no longer is our tenure. But it is not true. The poor ARE to be trusted in almost every situation where they have not been disunited from their natural superiors.

'Natural superiors' may make us wince, and it is true that though in his novels Scott could introduce stupid and ridiculous landed proprietors and contrast them with intelligent and dignified peasants, he did in his conscious political thinking believe in a natural order which put the landowner (ideally, benevolent, educated and responsible) at the head of local social groupings. But Scott's diagnosis of how things got the way they were sounds more modern:

> Formerly obliged to seek the sides of rapid streams for driving their machinery, manufacturers established themselves in sequestred spots and lodged their working people in villages around them. Hence arose a mutual dependence on each other between the employer & employd for in bad times the Master had to provide

61

for these peoples sustenance else he could not have their service in good & the little establishment naturally looked up to him as their head. But this has ceased since manufacturers have been transferd to great towns where a Master calls to- gether 100 workmen this week and pays them off the next with far less interest in their future fate than in that of as many worn-out shuttles.

This diagnosis puts Scott in line with the Victorian 'prophets' Carlyle, Ruskin and William Morris. It is worth remembering that the Industrial Revolution began in Scotland (on Clydeside) in Scott's youth. In deploring its social and moral effects while welcoming all possible technological aid for what Francis Bacon had called 'the relief of man's estate' Scott showed that he was caught up in a contradiction in which most of the great English writers of the nineteenth century were to be involved. It should be added, before this aspect of Scott is left, that he was personally a humane and generous man, kind and thoughtful to his own tenants at Abbotsford, with a great gift for commanding loyalty and affection from those who depended on him.

The military life   War with France brought alarums and excursions, and the fear of a French in- vasion encouraged the formation of volunteer forces. Scott took part with en- thusiasm in the formation of the Edinburgh Volunteer Light Dragoons in 1797. He became 'Paymaster, Quartermaster and Secretary' and was, as he put it himself, 'in consequence quite a military man'. In spite of his lameness he rode well, and he took part enthusiastically in the long daily drills. 'No fatigue ever seemed too much for him,' wrote a fellow officer later, 'and his zeal and animation served to sustain the enthusiasm of the whole corps. . . . At every interval of exercise, the order, *sit at ease*, was the signal for the quartermaster to lead the squadron to merri- ment; every eye was intuitively turned on "Earl Walter", as he was familiarly called by his associates at that date, and his ready joke seldom failed to raise the ready laugh.'

The Treaty of Amiens early in 1802 ended the war with France, but it broke out again in May 1803, and soon after, in Cockburn's words, 'Edinburgh, like every other place, became a camp, and continued so till the peace of 1814.' What Lock- hart called 'the volunteer mania in Scotland' broke out again and Scott again joined a volunteer force. Cockburn has given a classic account of Scott as a cavalryman:

Walter Scott's zeal in the cause was very curious. He was the soul of the Edin- burgh troop of Midlothian Yeomanry Cavalry. It was not a duty with him, or a necessity, or a pastime, but an absolute passion, intelligence in which grati- fied his feudal taste for war, and his jovial sociableness. He drilled, and drank, and made songs, with a hearty conscientious earnestness which inspired or shamed everybody within the attraction . . . his troop used to practise, individually, with the sabre-at a turnip, which was stuck on the top of a staff, to represent a Frenchman, in front of the line. Every other trooper, when he set forward in his turn, was far less concerned about the success of his aim at the turnip, than about how he was to tumble. But Walter pricked them forward gallantly, saying to himself, 'Cut them down, the villains, cut them down!' and made his blow, which from his lameness was often an awkward one, cordially, muttering curses all the while at the detested enemy.

Yet in some ways Cockburn's account is misleading. It is true that Scott was fasci-nated by war and armies. 'For myself,' he wrote to Anna Seward in 1803, 'I must own that to one who has like myself, *la tête un peu exaltée*, the "pomp and circum-stance of war" gives, for a time, a very poignant and pleasing sensation. The impos-ing appearance of cavalry, in particular, and the rush which marks the onset, appear to me to partake highly of the sublime. Perhaps I am the more attached to this sort of sport of swords, because my health requires much active exercise, and a lameness contracted in childhood renders it inconvenient for me to take it otherwise than on horseback.' He wrote often in this vein to correspondents, and he bought a com-mission in the 18th Regiment of Hussars for his son Walter, but at the same time he had no illusions about the soldier's life. 'I must say,' he wrote ironically to his sister-in-law Mrs Thomas Scott in 1825, 'it [soldiering] is a hopeful profession where a man buys an annuity on much worse terms than he could get it upon Change, binds himself to be a slave to the commands of others and occasionally to spoil his annuity bargain by putting himself in the way of being killed – and after all to be told he is very lucky & has got high promotion.' But the evidence of his novels is even more important. Nowhere in literature is there a more vivid presentation of the cruel senselessness of war. And the more 'romantic' the situation, the more stupid and meaningless the fighting becomes. A study of Scott's scenes of military violence, from the Battle of Prestonpans in *Waverley*, through the brutal pageantry of violence in *Ivanhoe*, the aimless Border fighting in *The Monastery* and the fatal swaggering and the final battle in *The Abbot*, to the last monstrous clan battle of *The Fair Maid of Perth*, will show what he really thinks of the panoply of war. It is all, in fact, in *Waverley*. It is only after Waverley has been separated from the Jacobite army by the ridiculous skirmish in Cumberland, and finds shelter with a peaceful farming family, Scott tells us, 'that the romance of his life was ended, and that its real history had now commenced'.

A final word on Scott's politics. All his life he remained a High Tory, and some-times he attacked the other side with virulence. But he was always aware of the personal accidents that had moulded his views. In January 1807, invited by a correspondent to deplore the death of the left-wing statesman Charles James Fox, he replied:

I was not only very early disposed to what have been called Tory principles by the opinions of those whom I respected & was bound to respect but the favour I received the intimacy in which I lived with many of Lord Melville's family his nephew & son in particular, was founded as much upon attachment to their measures in 1792–3 as to gratitude for favours received at a time when they were truly valuable. And so we will let that matter rest not only that I sympathize deeply in the loss of Mr Foxes high talents at a time when the country never needed them more & that I am candid enough to esteem the principles & cherish the [friendship] of many whose political opinions are different from my own, because I know they are adopted by those who hold them from an internal conviction of their rectitude.

He went further than this in writing to the dramatist Joanna Baillie in March 1810:

I wish I was like you in every thing, but politics in this free country make an early part of our education and become bone of our bone and flesh of our flesh. There is no difference except in words and personal predilections between the candid and well informed of both parties. In principle there is and can be none. . . .

And to Southey in September 1809:

I am convinced that what Swift said of Whig and Tory is true of most civil dissensions and that the really honest only require to know each other's sentiments to agree while knaves and fools invent catch-words and shibboleths and war-cries to keep them from coming to a just understanding.

The Battle of Bothwell Bridge, described so vividly by Scott in *Old Mortality*, resulted in total defeat of the Covenanters by an army commanded by the Duke of Monmouth

(*Left*) Miniature of Scott in the uniform of the Royal Edinburgh Light Dragoons. (*Right*) The playwright Joanna Baillie, regarded by Scott as the greatest dramatist since Shakespeare

This explains why Scott throughout his life could have warm friends and admirers among the Whigs (including Lord Cockburn): it also sums up a theme of many of his novels – almost, indeed, his philosophy of history – that it is the catch-words and war-cries, themselves both products and makers of history, that keep men of good-will apart. This is the voice of the Scott who is part of the Scottish Enlightenment rather than of Scott the early enthusiast for the heroic sentimentalities of German Romanticism. There was also Scott the Scottish Nationalist, and as we shall see he complicates the picture.

Scott took his bride to Edinburgh where after two temporary domiciles they settled at 39 North Castle Street, which Scott bought and retained as his Edinburgh residence until he had to sell it after the crash in 1826. He also bought a little cottage at the village of Lasswade, some six miles from Edinburgh on the River Esk: here he did his translations from Bürger and here he spent some of the pleasantest months of his early married life, remembering in later years how happy he had been building with his own hands garden walls and bowers. On 16 December 1799, through the Duke of Buccleuch's influence with Lord Melville, Scott was appointed Sheriff-depute of Selkirkshire, at an annual salary of £300. The duties of this judicial office in a small rural court (and he was assisted by a Sheriff-substitute) were, in Lockhart's words, 'far from heavy; the district, small, peaceful and pastoral, was in great part the property of the Duke of Buccleuch; and he turned with re-doubled zeal to his project of editing the ballads, many of the best of which belonged to this very district of his favourite Border.'

Scott's cottage, Lasswade, 'a small house, but with one room of good dimensions, which Mrs Scott's taste set off to advantage at very humble cost.' (Lockhart)

39 North Castle Street, Scott's Edinburgh house from late in 1801 until he had to sell it after his ruin in 1826

The actor Charles Mackay as Nicol Jarvie in the dramatized version of *Rob Roy*. Mackay, 'being himself a native of Glasgow, entered into the minutest peculiarities of the character with high *gusto*, and gave the west country dialect in its most racy perfection'. (Lockhart)

By 1800 Scott was in the full tide of his editorial work on the ballads. Assisted by the learned Richard Heber and the remarkable self-educated scholar John Leyden, he read and collected and discussed and corresponded and steadily built up the background of knowledge necessary to produce the historical and explanatory notes and references with which the collection was garnished. The first two volumes appeared early in 1802, and the third volume the following year. His Introduction ends with a significant paragraph:

> In the Notes and occasional Dissertations, it has been my object to throw together, perhaps without sufficient attention to method, a variety of remarks, regarding popular superstitions, and legendary history, which, if not now collected, must soon have been totally forgotten. By such efforts, feeble as they are, I may contribute somewhat to the history of my native country; the peculiar features of whose manners and character are daily melting and dissolving into those of her sister and ally. And, trivial as may appear such an offering, to the manes of a kingdom, once proud and independent, I hang it upon her altar with a mixture of feelings, which I shall not attempt to describe.

The mixture of feelings is understandable. Scott supported the Union of 1707, and would certainly have endorsed Bailie Nicol Jarvie's defence of it in *Rob Roy* as having opened the English colonies to Glasgow traders among other commercial benefits. Yet he regretted Scotland's lost independence, and he cherished every surviving institution that suggested that it was not lost. At the same time he was a warm supporter of Henry Dundas, who virtually ruled Scotland on behalf of the

George IV at Holyrood House presented with the palace keys by the Duke of Hamilton

George IV, the
English-Irish-
Highlander

Westminster Government and who is regarded by modern Scottish Nationalists as a Quisling. Yet in a letter to Miss Clephane of 13 July 1813 he actually talked of his 'loyalty' to the exiled and by now long-impotent Stuarts, though he went on to explain the conflict between his head and his heart: 'I am very glad I did not live in 1745 for though as a lawyer I could not have pleaded Charles's right and as a clergyman I could not have prayed for him yet as a soldier I would I am sure against the convictions of my better reason have fought for him even to the bottom of the gallows.' Scott was active in the recovery of the long-concealed Scottish regalia, impotent reminder of the days of an independent Scottish kingdom, and at the same time he was responsible for George IV's visit to Scotland in 1822, a visit which he stage-managed and during which he succeeded in presenting the Hanoverian King, dressed in the kilt, as the rightful monarch of the Highland clansmen.

In 1806, as Cockburn put it, 'the Whigs were surprised to find themselves in power' and Scott feared, in Lockhart's words, 'that the new rulers of the country were disposed to abolish many of its valuable institutions'. Many reforms were long overdue in Scottish institutions, but Scott suspected reform, out of Scottish Nationalist feeling. There is a significant incident recorded by Lockhart:

At a debate of the Faculty of Advocates on some of these propositions [for certain innovations in Scottish legal procedures], he made a speech much longer than any he had ever before delivered in that assembly; and several who heard it have assured me, that it had a flow and energy of eloquence for which those who

68

knew him best had been quite unprepared. When the meeting broke up, he walked across *the Mound*, on his way to Castle Street, between Mr Jeffrey and another of his reforming friends, who complimented him on the rhetorical powers he had been displaying, and would willingly have treated the subject matter of the discussion playfully. But his feelings had been moved to an extent far beyond their apprehension: he exclaimed, 'No, no – 'tis no laughing matter; little by little, whatever your wishes may be, you will destroy and undermine, until nothing of what makes Scotland Scotland shall remain.' And so saying, he turned round to conceal his agitation – but not until Mr Jeffrey saw tears gushing down his cheek – resting his head until he recovered himself on the wall of the Mound.

Continuity – the unbroken line from past to present – the sense of oneness with earlier generations: these were central in Scott's feelings. At the same time he knew that in many important respects change was not only essential but highly desirable. Darsie Latimer in *Redgauntlet*, who so often speaks for Scott and is indeed modelled on himself, tells his sister that in the second decade after the defeat of the Forty-five Rebellion it would be vain to expect the tenants of a Jacobite laird to 'think of subjecting their necks again to the feudal yoke, which was effectually broken by the Act of 1748, abolishing vassalage and hereditary jurisdiction'. The Hereditary Jurisdictions Act, of which Scott approved, curbed the virtually absolute powers over their tenants previously possessed by Highland landlords and destroyed that very paternalism which, in a softer form, Scott sighed after and tried to practise at Abbotsford. As for Scott's 'loyalty' to the Stuarts, *Redgauntlet* exposes loyalty to the Stuart cause as an anachronistic and irrelevant sentimentality in the real world of the second half of the eighteenth century – part of *Redgauntlet*'s greatness as a novel lies in Scott's ability to expose Jacobitism without diminishing its heroic appeal – and in his *Journal* on 20 October 1826, after a pleasant visit with George IV, he commits himself fully to the kind of king required by the modern world:

The Deputy Ranger's House (The Royal Lodge), Windsor Great Park

He [George IV] is, in many respects, the model of a British monarch – has little inclination to try experiments on government otherwise than through his ministers – sincerely, I believe, desires the good of his subjects, is kind toward the distressed, and moves and speaks 'every inch a king'. I am sure such a character is fitter for us than a man who would long to head armies, or be perpetually intermeddling with *la grande politique*.

No wonder, then, that, in presenting his poetic monuments to an older, rougher and more violent way of life than the Scotland of his own day afforded, Scott spoke of his 'mixture of feeling'.

'The Minstrelsy'   *The Minstrelsy of the Scottish Border* contains many of the great Scottish ballads, including 'Sir Patrick Spens', 'Johnie Armstrang', 'The Battle of Otterbourne', 'The Twa Corbies', 'Lord Randal', 'A Lyke-Wake Dirge', 'The Wife of Usher's Well'. It presented them in an attractive form, with helpful notes, and in a text which Scott had undoubtedly occasionally 'improved' ('The Twa Corbies', for example). He went to great lengths to get texts, often from oral recitation, but his generation did not have the scrupulous respect for the text in the state in which they found it that modern scholars have and Scott considered himself fully justified in silently smoothing out a stanza or indeed providing expressions of greater tragic sonority than the original. In a letter of 1806 he denied 'interpolating these ancient Ballads' and mentioned the sources of some of his 'original copies'; but there can be no doubt that his hand is in some of the texts he presented, though more often by the conflation of different texts than by the substitution of original material.

The Minstrelsy, wrote Scott to his brother-in-law Charles Carpenter in March 1803, 'was so well received by a *discerning* public that after receiving £100 profit for the first edition, which my vanity cannot omit informing you sold off in six months, I sold the copyright for £500 more'. There were numerous later editions, especially after Scott had achieved fame as a poet in his own right. And this was the direction in which he was now heading. Not that Scott ever gave up his editing and miscellaneous historical and antiquarian writing: he kept these up throughout his life. He spent much time in 1803 and 1804 on his edition of the medieval romance *Sir Tristrem*, which was published in 1804. At the same time he was working on a poem of his own, a 'romance of Border chivalry', which was originally intended for the third volume of *The Minstrelsy*, containing 'imitations of the ancient ballad'. The theme had been suggested to him by 'the lovely young Countess of Dalkieth', later Harriet, Duchess of Buccleuch, whom Scott respected and adored and whose death in 1814 prostrated him. The Countess 'enjoined' on Scott the task of writing a ballad on the Border legend of Gilpin Horner. He chose a metre and stanza form suggested by Coleridge's *Christabel*, which he much admired. The 'ballad' eventually emerged as a long narrative poem in six cantos, *The Lay of the Last*

Illustration to *The Lay of the Last Minstrel* by Scott's great friend Sir William Allan

Minstrel, which was published in January 1805. It was an immediate and enormous success, a fact which, as Lockhart put it, 'at once decided that literature should form the main business of Scott's life'.

Things were going well for Scott. In 1804 his uncle Captain Robert Scott of Kelso had died, leaving Rosebank and thirty acres of good pastoral land to Walter. He sold the house and land for £5,000, and received a further £600 from the residue of his uncle's estate. Apart from his literary earnings he now had a fixed income of nearly £1,000 a year. He had already decided to give up his 'sweet little cottage on the banks of the Esk' and seek a more suitable residence in his Sheriffdom, where anyway by law he was supposed to be residing. So in the summer of 1804 he rented the small country-house of Ashestiel, most attractively situated on the southern bank of the Tweed a few miles from Selkirk, and this became his country quarters until he bought Abbotsford in 1812. At the time of the move to Ashestiel the Scotts were the parents of three children, Sophia, born in 1799, Walter, born in 1801 and Anne, born in 1803. Their youngest, Charles, was born the day before Christmas 1805.

The Minstrelsy had been published by 'the respectable house of Cadell Davies, in the Strand', and printed, by Scott's arranging, by his old schoolfellow James Ballantyne, now the successful proprietor of the *Kelso Mail* and a printer of style and accuracy. 'When the book came out,' Scott later recalled, 'the imprint, Kelso,

A business partner

71

Ashestiel, 'a decent
farmhouse overhanging the
Tweed'; (*left*) as sketched by
Turner, (*below*) as it is today

was read with wonder by amateurs of typography, who had never heard of such a place, and were astonished at the example of handsome printing which so obscure a town had produced.' As early as 1800 Scott had urged Ballantyne to move to Edinburgh, but Ballantyne took his time. Finally, in 1802, leaving the paper to the management of his youngest brother Sandy, he set up his presses in two rooms at Abbeyhill, near Holyrood, but because of the amount of legal printing that Scott was able to steer his way, this soon became too small and he moved first to Foulis Close in the Canongate and then to much larger premises in Paul's Work at the North Back of the Canongate near the foot of Leith Wynd.

The first edition of *The Lay of the Last Minstrel* was published by Longman, Hurst, Rees, and Orme in London (who had also published the second edition and the third volume of *The Minstrelsy* in 1803) and printed by Ballantyne, who also acted as a most meticulous proof-reader, a role he had played for *The Minstrelsy* and was

Paul's Work, where James
Ballantyne finally established his press
in Edinburgh

to continue to play for Scott almost to the end of the latter's life. But the Edinburgh publisher Archibald Constable had been watching Scott's literary fortunes with interest. He had already bought a quarter share of *The Minstrelsy* and had published *Sir Tristrem*. Now he bought from Longman a quarter share of *The Lay*. So both Constable and Ballantyne, fateful names in Scott's subsequent financial history, had already become involved in his life.

Archibald Constable, born in 1774, had begun his career as a bookseller's apprentice in Edinburgh in 1788; then became a bookseller in his own right; and finally became also a publisher. He had started *The Edinburgh Review* in 1802, and speedily made it an enormous success. There had been nothing like Constable in Scottish – or for that matter in English – publishing. 'Abandoning the old timid and grudging system,' wrote Cockburn, 'Constable stood out as the general patron of all promising publications, and confounded not merely his rivals in trade, but his very authors, by his unheard-of prices. Ten, even twenty, guineas a sheet for a review, £2000 or £3000 for a single poem, and £1000 each for two philosophical dissertations, drew authors from dens where they would otherwise have starved, and made Edinburgh a literary mart, famous with strangers, and the pride of its own citizens.'

The success of *The Lay* put pressure on James Ballantyne's resources. To meet the demand he had to hold up other printing orders. New equipment was also necessary. He turned to Scott for help, and his appeal came at a propitious time. Though Scott had not decided to make literature his main profession – it was to be his staff but not his crutch, he said – he was clearly going to devote a considerable amount of his time to it, and, if the auguries were to be trusted, profitably. He still had the bulk of his uncle's legacy untouched. If he could get printing commissions for Ballantyne – not only his own work, but masses of legal printing and the reprinting of all sorts of antiquarian and historical works with which Scott's brain teemed and which he was sure publishers would jump at – then Ballantyne, who was a first-rate printer, was bound to do well. Scott liked the idea of secretly being the power behind the throne in Ballantyne's printing business. And he hoped to make a lot of money. The upshot was that in May 1805 he signed a partnership agreement with Ballantyne. He had already lent the printer £500 on his moving to Edinburgh; now he advanced another £1,500 and it was agreed that Ballantyne, the active partner, should receive one-third of the profits with the remaining two-thirds divided between the partners in proportion to their stock, which in fact meant in almost equal shares.

Scott's next step was to try to interest publishers in grandiose publishing schemes which would, of course, have to be printed by Ballantyne. The most impressive of these – an edition of the British poets in over a hundred volumes – fell through. More successful was the plan for an eighteen-volume edition of Dryden, edited by

74

(*Left*) Archibald Constable, whom Scott described as a 'prince of booksellers [i.e. publishers].'
(*Right*) John Ballantyne, titular head of John Ballantyne & Co., booksellers and publishers

Scott; he managed to persuade the London publisher William Miller to undertake this, on the condition that Ballantyne got the printing order. Scott now entered on a period of frenzied editing: not only the Dryden, which involved a huge amount of work, but seventeenth-century memoirs, early tracts, miscellaneous antiquarian works of various kinds. He did the work with a kind of negligent ease, drawing on his vast reading and his copious memory. The various publishers whom he persuaded to take on these works seldom made much, if anything, out of them. But Ballantyne always got the printing, and Scott could always be sure of one-third of Ballantyne's profits. And of course he shared Ballantyne's risks.

In 1809 Scott plunged further into the world of business. He was responsible for the founding of the firm of John Ballantyne & Co., booksellers and publishers, in which the partners were Scott himself, James Ballantyne and his younger brother John. Scott's share of the profits was one-half and that of each of the brothers one-quarter. This was the result of a quarrel with Constable, or rather with his somewhat stiff-necked partner Alexander Gibson Hunter. Scott was going to show Constable: he would set up a rival firm which would outdo the roaringly successful Edinburgh publisher at his own game. Scott had the last word in the direction of the publishing firm, though John Ballantyne was the titular head. At the same time Scott renegotiated his partnership agreement with James with respect to the printing firm – which continued to exist – so as to give Scott and James Ballantyne one-half each of the company's assets (valued at £7,684), with a 'divisible profit on trade' of

£1,350 annually, of which two-thirds (£900) went to James and one-third (£450) to Scott. A minute appended to the agreement reconstituted the firm's capital at £6,000, each partner having £3,000 stock, and stipulated that any partner who put more than his share of the capital in the company's funds should receive 'on such advance a trade profit of fifteen per cent'. Scott then went on to invest a total of £3,000 in the printing firm, on which he was able to make an annual £450, representing interest at the agreed but extraordinarily high rate of 15 per cent.

But things did not go smoothly. The firm of John Ballantyne & Co., loaded with unsaleable antiquarian works for which Scott but nobody else was enthusiastic, ran into deep trouble, and in 1813 it was arranged for it to be wound up, though the printing business of James Ballantyne & Co. carried on. It was Constable who rescued John Ballantyne & Co., not altogether disinterestedly because, of course, he wanted Scott – now an immensely popular best-selling author – back on his list. So he bought up part of John Ballantyne's stock and in other ways eased the last days of the firm. The printing firm continued, becoming more and more in Scott's debt until in 1816 it was agreed that it should be carried on for Scott's behoof alone, with James as salaried manager; James was reassumed as partner in 1822, and so the firm went on until it stopped payment on the fatal day of 17 January 1826. This outline story is given here so that Scott's subsequent career can be related to it.

Profession and literature

We return to Scott at Ashestiel, throwing himself with zest into his edition of Dryden. In his frequent correspondence with his older friend George Ellis – editor, historian, essayist, and founder of the *Anti-Jacobin* together with the statesman and man of letters George Canning, another of Scott's friends and correspondents – we get a rich running commentary on his literary activities and interests at this time. In October 1805 Ellis wrote to Scott about the problem posed by the indecencies perpetrated by Dryden in his comedies and elsewhere. 'I must own that the announcement of a *general* edition of Dryden gave me some alarm,' he wrote, but Scott resisted any suggestion of bowdlerizing the older poet:

I will not castrate John Dryden. I would as soon castrate my own father, as I believe Jupiter did of yore. What would you say to any man who could castrate Shakespeare, or Massinger, or Beaumont and Fletcher? . . . it is not passages of ludicrous indelicacy that corrupt the manners of a people – it is the sonnets which a prurient genius like Master Little [Thomas Moore; but later Scott became good friends with him] sings *virginibus puerisque* – it is the sentimental slang, half lewd, half methodistic, that debauches the understanding, inflames the sleeping passions, and prepares the reader to give way as soon as a tempter appears.

A letter to Ellis of 25 January 1806 throws light on other aspects of Scott's activities:

You must know . . . that with a view of withdrawing entirely at the bar, I had entered into a transaction with an elderly and infirm gentleman, Mr George

76

Home, to be associated with him in the office which he holds as one of the principal clerks to our supreme Court of Session; I being to discharge the duty gratuitously during his life, and to suceed him at his decease. . . . By the interest of my kind and noble friend, the Duke of Buccleuch, the countenance of Govern-ment was obtained to this arrangement, and the affair, as I have every reason to believe, is now in the Treasury . . . the news of to-day giving us every reason to apprehend Pitt's death, if that lamentable event has not already happened [it had; on the twenty-third], makes me get nervous on a subject so interesting to my little fortune. My political sentiments have always been constitutional and open, and although they were never rancorous, yet I cannot expect that the Scottish Opposi-tion party, should circumstances bring them into power, would consider me as an object of favour: nor would I ask it at their hands. Their leaders cannot re-gard me with malevolence, for I am intimate with many of them; but they must provide for the Whiggish children before they throw their bread to the Tory dogs; and I shall not fawn on them because they have in their turn the superintendence of the larder.

Scott is trying to insure himself against the possible loss of patronage in the event of a change of government. The Clerkship of Session, he goes on, is worth £800 a year, and if he agrees to perform the duties for nothing until Home dies (Home enjoying the salary for as long as he lives), he will then be guaranteed that salary. As for the job itself, 'the duty consists in a few hours' labour in the forenoons when the Court sits,

A health to Lord Melville, a song included by Scott in a letter to Robert Dundas, 1806

A

HEALTH TO LORD MELVILLE;

BEING

AN EXCELLENT NEW SONG.

Were they not forced with those that should be ours,
We might have met them dareful, beard to beard,
d beat ?　　　　　　　　　　SHAKESPEARE.

Air—*Carrickfergus.*

Since here we are set in array round the table,
　　Five hundred good fellows well met in a hall;
Come listen, brave boys, and I'll sing as I'm able,
　　How Innocence triumph'd, and Pride got a fall.
　　　　But push round the claret;
　　　　Come, stewards, don't spare it,
　th rapture you'l　　　to the toasts that I　.
　　　　Here, b^ys,
　　　　Off with it merrily,
Melville for ever, and long may he live.

leaving the evenings and whole vacation open for literary pursuits.' The new Government behaved more handsomely than Scott expected: in April 1806 Scott wrote to Southey that he had been 'fortunate enough notwithstanding the change of men and measures to secure the reversion of a considerable patent office which was destined for me by W. Pitt and Lord Melville . . . it is particularly acceptable to me as it enables me without imprudence or indeed injustice to my family to retire from the bar which I have always thought and felt to be an irksome and even hateful profession.' Unfortunately, George Home did not die soon, as everyone expected, and a rather tragi-comic situation arose, with Scott coming more and more to regard Home's refusal to die as a personal affront. He was an Old Man of the Sea whom he could not get rid of. Throughout 1811 he bombarded his influential friends with letters pointing out that he had been doing the work for nothing for five years and some new arrangement ought to be made to enable him to draw the salary. He wrote again and again to Lord Melville, even more frequently to Lady Abercorn, and once to Robert Dundas. One of his first letters on the subject to Lady Abercorn ends:

On the whole if your Ladyship expects any more harmony from me you must take my case into your kind consideration recollecting always that I am only craving to be promoted to the emoluments of situation [sic] of which I have held the rank & discharged the duty gratis for five years compleat, & which I believe no one will say is much disproportioned to my birth expectations or standing in Society. . . .

But it was not until January 1812 (with the Old Man of the Sea still alive) that the business was settled to Scott's satisfaction; he was to receive a salary of £1,300 which, as he wrote to Lady Abercorn, 'makes my circumstances very easy & even affluent. In fact as our former income afforded us all the comforts & some of the elegancies of life & as neither my wife nor I have the least wish to step beyond the decent & hospitable expence we have hitherto been able to maintain an addition which raises our income from £1,500 to £2,800 is in truth a little mine of wealth which prudently husbanded will prevent, if it please God to spare me a few years, the anxious feelings which a parent must entertain in my circumstances concerning those who are to succeed him.'

As one of the six Clerks to the Court of Session Scott had duties which were largely routine, but which kept him in Edinburgh when the Court was in session (i.e. from 12 November to 12 March and from 12 May to 12 July, with three weeks break at Christmas-time). Later on he was accused of having written some of his novels in Court, but this he indignantly denied. He certainly did write many letters in Court, often mentioning the fact to his correspondent, sometimes actually describing the scene, with the judge droning on behind him. Attendance was on

Sketch of Scott as Clerk of the Court of
Session by Mark Napier

week-days except Mondays and alternate Wednesdays, for about four hours from
10 a.m. but up to six hours on especially busy days. He frequently described the
work as light: he told the poet Crabbe that it was 'neither laborious nor requiring
exertions of the mind'. But he did call the work 'laborious' when writing to Lady
Abercorn to ask her to use her influence with Lord Melville to enable him to draw
the emoluments of the office.

In 1808 Scott was writing to Lady Abercorn to ask her to use her influence in
high places, this time to secure for him the secretaryship of a Parliamentary Com-
mission to look into all forms of jurisprudence in Scotland. 'You see my dear
friend,' he concludes, 'how little I fear wearying your kindness on my behalf –
& I am sure that it will give you pleasure to think that my prospects are opening
fairly & that those who have best opportunity to see me as a man of business do not
find my poetical excursions disqualifying me for the serious pursuits of life.' He
got the job, which was remunerative, and worked hard at preparing the Com-
mission's report at the end of December 1809 and the beginning of January 1810.
'The poor Secretary has hardly a moment to call his own from nine in the morning
till the same hour at night,' he wrote to Lady Abercorn on 31 December 1809.
This work interrupted the composition of *The Lady of the Lake*, his third major
narrative poem, which appeared in May 1810. The second, *Marmion*, had appeared
in 1808. *The Lady of the Lake* represented the peak of Scott's popularity as a poet.
Though he published a number of other narrative poems – *Rokeby* and (anonymously, to mystify the critics) *The Bridal of Triermain* in 1813, *The Lord of the Isles*
in 1815 – he knew that after Byron entered the field with the first two cantos of

Childe Harold's Pilgrimage in 1812 he could not compete for public favour with Byron's more dashing manner. Scott's kind of romantic narrative was not spiced with the special combination of self-pity, *bravura* and calculated moral ambiguity which made the Byronic hero such a potent force in European literature. He ceded the field gracefully, and though Byron had in his satirical *English Bards and Scotch Reviewers* (1809) attacked Scott for following a mercenary muse, the two later corresponded in terms of high heroic friendship, then met and cemented their friendship further. They lived in different moral and political worlds, yet each understood and admired the other.

More business commitments

Scott's edition of Dryden, in its massive eighteen volumes, was published in 1808; the editor's fee of forty guineas a volume earned him £756. It is characteristic of Scott's literary production at this time that *Marmion* appeared a couple of months before the Dryden, having been written while he was working on the final stages of the latter work. He was now in a position, which he relished, to play one publisher off against another. Constable offered Scott 1,000 guineas for *Marmion* before he had seen a line of it, and Scott accepted. Constable sold one-fourth of the copyright to William Miller and another to John Murray, both of London. (The reason why Scott jumped at the offer of 1,000 guineas outright in advance, was that he needed money to help his brother Thomas. Thomas had – evidently through inefficiency rather than criminality – misappropriated rents when he was factor or agent for Lord Abercorn, and Scott had to be prepared to make good the loss so caused and do what he could for his brother, whom he helped continually in one way or another for as long as he lived, and whose widow he helped after Tom's death: he also looked after and launched into the world Tom's son, his nephew, also called Walter. If Scott was fond of money it must be remembered that he was also extremely generous, and had a very deep sense of family solidarity which put his purse at the disposal of his relatives whenever there was real need.)

Ring given to Scott on the death of Byron

Constable was anxious not to lose Scott. When Scott had finished his Dryden Constable proposed an edition of Swift on the same scale at double the rate of payment which Miller had given for the Dryden. This meant £1,500, and Scott accepted. But the Swift project seemed to inaugurate a period of increasing difficulty with Constable, and there were many arguments and interruptions before it finally appeared in 1814. Part of the trouble was political. Constable, as publisher of the influential Whig periodical *The Edinburgh Review*, was held responsible for the views it expressed. In April 1808 *The Edinburgh*'s editor, Francis Jeffrey, published a long review of *Marmion* which was decidedly cool. ('To write a modern romance of chivalry, seems to be much such a phantasy as to build a modern abbey or an English pagoda. For once, however, it may be excused as a pretty caprice of genius; but a second production of the same sort is entitled to less indulgence, and imposes a sort of duty to drive the author from so idle a task, by a

80

Byron in the Highlands

fair exposition of the faults which are, in a manner, inseparable from its execution.') Scott refused to take umbrage at this, and Jeffrey dined with the Scotts just after the appearance of the review (but Charlotte was annoyed). The next issue of *The Edinburgh Review*, however, contained an article on the Spanish situation which Scott considered politically intolerable, and he wrote to Constable saying that he could no longer continue to be a contributor. Scott now concerned himself actively with the foundation of a rival review, as Tory as *The Edinburgh* was Whig, and this, *The Quarterly Review*, started publication in London in February with John Murray as publisher and William Gifford as editor. Though Scott himself hated the expression of party bitterness in periodicals and especially hated offensive anonymous reviews, and proposed for *The Quarterly* a policy of courtesy and generosity, it soon developed a reputation for no-holds-barred reviewing on political lines, and in 1818 published the most notorious of such reviews, John Wilson Croker's savage attack on Keats and his *Endymion*, an attack which was popularly but erroneously supposed to have hastened Keats's death.

Scott's annoyance with *The Edinburgh* and association with the new *Quarterly* would not itself have caused a breach with Constable, though it did not improve the atmosphere. Constable's associate Hunter disapproved of the large sum Constable had given for the Swift edition and expressed the wish that Scott, having been so well paid, should concentrate on that and not dissipate his energies on so many different projects. Scott was offended, and wrote offering to give up the Swift contract, an offer which Constable refused. But Scott was not mollified, and wrote a stiff letter, not to Constable himself but to the firm, formalizing the quarrel. Perhaps Scott was really looking for an excuse for a breach with Constable, so that he could set up John Ballantyne as his rival. Anyway, this is what he did. *The Lady of the Lake* was published by John Ballantyne & Co., with one-quarter share purchased by Miller of London. Scott's author's fee of 2,000 guineas was of course augmented by his share in the profits as partner of the publishing firm as well as by his share as partner in the firm of James Ballantyne, printers. The first edition, a quarto edition of 2,050 copies, was sold out immediately on publication, and four octavo editions appeared in the course of the same year, bringing the total sales to 20,000 within a few months. Many more editions followed.

'The Lady of the Lake'

Evidence of the work's success is given by the publisher Cadell, who later became a partner of Constable and finally acquired the firm after Constable's bankruptcy. Cadell was then a young trainee publisher in Edinburgh. Looking back in later life, he recalled the 'extraordinary sensation' caused by the publication of the poem:

> The whole country rang with the praises of the poet – crowds set off to the scenery of Loch Katrine, till then comparatively unknown; and as the book came out just before the season for excursions, every house and inn in that neighbourhood was crammed with a constant succession of visitors. It is a well-ascertained fact, that from the date of the publication of *The Lady of the Lake* the post-horse duty in Scotland rose in an extraordinary degree, and indeed it continued to do so regularly for a number of years, the author's succeeding works keeping up the enthusiasm for our scenery which he had thus originally created.

Loch Katrine, from the west end

View of Abbotsford through the gateway, 1832

Tourists from the south had of course visited the Highlands before Scott – indeed as early as July 1810 Scott, with considerable exaggeration, called the age one in which 'every London citizen makes Loch Lomond his washpot and throws his shoe over Ben Nevis' – but it was Scott who made touring, first in the Trossachs and then in other parts of the Highlands, a really popular activity. After the defeat of the Jacobite Rebellion in 1746 the Highlands were closely supervised and many Highland customs proscribed; later came economic horrors and the Highland clearances. Scott's aim in much of his writing was a healing one: to present the glamour of Scottish history and landscape, with the heroic violence that made part of the glamour modulated quietly into the past tense, so that Scotland could be seen as now part of a peaceful and enlightened Britain. It is in a sense all summed up in Abbotsford, his great mansion in the Scottish Baronial style, with its fantastic collection of relics of the heroic past – armour, weapons, relics of all kinds from warriors and bandits, heraldic blazonings – together with its ultra-modern gas lighting, its patent stove 'with a communication for ventilating in the summer' and its wonderful (but in the end unsuccessful) new kind of air bell, working by compression, 'with neither wire nor crank of any kind', as Scott proudly told a correspondent.

Scott's narrative poetry is often facile, and sometimes trots on in a dogged and predictable cadence that soon wearies the ear. But at its best it has movement, life, and a tremendous feeling for the relation of lively incident to its scenic background. And in those autobiographical interludes in *Marmion* Scott gives the reader, in a

Air compression bell, still functioning, in the drawing-room at Abbotsford

William Erskine, 'the chief literary confidant and counsellor' of Scott's mature years

fluent, unaffected, vivid and really moving way, an account of the development of his own sensibility which compares favourably with the 'growth of a poet's mind' in Wordsworth's *Prelude*. In incidental lyrics in the poems – as later in the novels – Scott captured a variety of ballad and folk styles with real brilliance and also revealed a striking lyrical strain of his own. Further, the poems have some great dramatic moments, some memorable action scenes, and some set descriptive pieces (such as the stag fleeing the hunt at the opening of *The Lady of the Lake*) which, once read, stay permanently in the mind. So we need not be surprised at Scott's great popularity as a poet at the end of the first and beginning of the second decade of the nineteenth century, nor that he was offered (and declined) the Poet Laureateship in 1813.

Scott never really knew where he was going in his literary career. He played everything by ear, and regarded most of his writing as impromptus which luckily hit the public taste. In October 1808 he wrote to George Ellis: 'I have done with poetry for some time – it is a scourging crop and ought not to be hastily repeated. Editing, therefore, may be considered a green crop of turnips and peas, . . . Swift is my *grande opus* at present.' But in fact he went on writing narrative poems until Byron outbid him in public favour. Then, accidentally discovering in 1813 a prose novel he had begun in 1805 but had soon laid aside because of adverse criticism of its opening chapters by William Erskine, he decided to go ahead with it. It was all a matter of pure chance, as Scott himself explained in his General Preface. 'I happened to want some fishing-tackle for the use of a guest [at Abbotsford], when it occurred to me to search the old writing-desk . . . in which I used to keep articles of that nature. I got access to it with some difficulty; and, in looking for lines and flies, the long-lost manuscript presented itself; I immediately set to work to complete it, according to my original purpose.'

Manuscript of *Waverley* ▶

Waverley — not so portly yet as my old friend Sir Everard — mais cela viendra avec le tems, as my good acquaintance Ba: -ron Kikkitbroeck said of the Sagesse etc "Madame son Epouse — And so ye have mounted the cockade — right right — Though he could have wished the colour different — & I would hae' deemed Sir Eve :-rard — but no more of that I am old and times are changed and how does the worthy knight baronet and the fair Mrs Rachael — ah ye laugh young man but she was the fair fair Mrs Rachael in the year of Grace Seventeen hundred and sixteen — But tiem passes — et singula praedantur anni — that is most certain. But once again ye are most heartily welcome to my poor house of Tully Veolan. Hie to the house Rose and see that John Culbertson looks out the old Chateau Margoux which I sent from Bourdeaux to Dundee in the year 1713 the we cannot rival the luxuries of your English table Captain Waverley or give you the Epula lautiores of Waverley Honor — I say Epula rather than prandium because the latter latter phrase is popular — prandium Epula ad senatum vero prandium, ad populam attinet says Suetonius Tranquillus — But I trust ye will supplaud, my Bourdeaux, c'est des deux oreilles as Capt Vinsauf used to say — Vinum primae notae the Principal of St. Andrews denominated it and once more Captain Waverley glad I am I that ye are here to drink the best my cellar can make forth-coming." Thus spake with the necessary interjectional answers continued from the lower ally when they met up to the door of the house where four or five servants in old-fashioned liveries headed by John Culbertson & the Butler who now bore no token of the sable stains of the garden received them en grand costume with much ceri=mony and still more real kindness the Baron without stopping in any intermediate apartment conducted his guest through worse into great dining parlour where a table was set forth in form for six persons & an old-fashioned buffet displayed all the ancient and massive plate of the Bradwardine family. A bell was now heard at the head of the avenue for an old man who acted as porter upon gala days had caught the alarm &

Abbotsford   By this time Scott and his family were settled at Abbotsford. His lease at Ashestiel ran out in May 1811 and he looked around for a place to buy. At first it was just for 'a piece of ground sufficient for a cottage & a few fields'. On 1 July 1811 he wrote to his friend the traveller and classical scholar J. B. S. Morritt of Rokeby that he had 'bought a small farm value about £150 yearly with the intention of "bigging myself a tower" after my own fashion. The situation is good as it lies along the Tweed about three miles above Melrose but alas! the plantations are very young. However I think if I can get an elegant plan for a cottage it will look very well, . . .' The idea of owning his own property delighted him. 'Now I am a *Laird*,' he wrote to Lady Abercorn. His letters to his friends in the summer of 1811 are filled with his plans for enlarging both the property and the building. He plants trees like mad, this being an absolute passion with him all his life. He adds to his collection of heroic relics. 'I have been ruining myself by the purchase of a small lot of ancient armour and other curiosities (Rob Roy's gun among other things)', is a typical observation in a letter. In January 1812 he is writing to Joanna Baillie: 'I fear I shall want a great deal of money to make my cottage what I should like it.' The story of Abbotsford would make a book.

Melrose, by Turner. Abbotsford lies about three miles above the famous abbey

Clarty Hole, 1812, the original farmhouse on the Abbotsford site was, according to Lockhart, 'small and poor'

Two views of Abbotsford, the 'cottage' on which he expended such vast sums

(*Above*) A hill run with the Duke of Buccleuch's hounds

Rhymer's Glen the 'strange secluded ravine' on the boundary of the Abbotsford estate named by Scott for its association with the thirteenth-century Scottish seer and poet Thomas the Rhymer

Bust of Scott
by Chantrey

(*Below*) Abbotsford, from the
northern bank of the Tweed, with
the Scott family picnicking in the
foreground: Turner

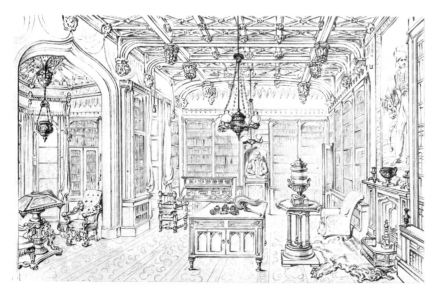

Abbotsford:
the library

(*Below left*) Catalogue of a collection of military antiquities. Scott could never resist catalogues such as these. He would commission the actor Daniel Terry in London to buy antiquities for him and used them to decorate his rooms such as the entrance hall (*below right*)

GOTHIC HALL, PALL MALL.

CATALOGUE

OF A SPLENDID COLLECTION OF

Military Antiquities,

COMPRISING

*The most rare and interesting Specimens of Arms & Armour
from the*

NORMAN CONQUEST,

TO THE LATEST PERIODS.

Including numerous examples of the most beautiful and exquisite Workmanship
IN NOBLE
SHIELDS, HELMETS, SWORDS, GUNS, &c. &c.
By the celebrated BENVENUTI CELLINI, and other eminent Artists, &c. &c.

Among the Royal and most distinguished Suits in this

COLLECTION

WILL BE FOUND—THE ANTIENT CRUSADER!

KNIGHTS mounted for the Tournament,

(UPON THEIR NOBLE STEEDS)

The renowned ALBERT, the Giant of Bavaria,

HENRY IV. of FRANCE,

&c. &c. &c.

*The whole forming a display, whic for magnificence, interest and amuseme t,
is allowed to surpass every thing of the kind in Europe!*

THE FOURTH EDITION WITH ADDITIONS.

London:

PRINTED BY J. DAVY, QUEEN STREET, SEVEN DIALS.

1819.

Abbotsford today

Scott kept buying up neighbouring property – Abbotslee in 1812 for £4,000 and Kaeside in 1816, which he bought with a mortgage for £3,000, a mortgage he did not pay off until just before the crash of 1826, when he borrowed £10,000 on the Abbotsford estate, using £3,000 to repay the Kaeside mortgage. Writing to Joanna Baillie in November 1815 he proudly signed himself 'Abbotsford and Kaeside'. In December 1816 he is writing: 'I have enlarged my dominions here not greatly in extent, but infinitely in point of beauty, as my boundary is now a strange secluded ravine full of old thorne trees, hazels, guelder roses, willows, and so forth, with a dashing rivulet.' In October 1817 he writes: 'I have bought a good farm adjacent to Abbotsford and beautifully situated so I am now a considerable Laird and Walter [his son] may be a rich one if he is prudent and regulated.' This was the fine estate of Toftfield (now renamed Huntly Burn), which Scott bought for £10,000, settling his friend Adam Ferguson in the new house there. On the very eve of the great financial crash of 1826 he was planning a vast extension to his estates, although in May 1825 he had written ironically to his sister-in-law Mrs Thomas Scott that 'the real road to ruin is . . . to have an improveable estate with a taste for building.' It turned out to be the literal truth for him.

But it was the house rather than the land that really captured his imagination. The modest cottage grew and grew and grew. In January 1818, in a letter to the Duke of Buccleuch, he called it 'a Dalilah of my imagination'. 'Builders and planners have drained my purse,' he wrote to Joanna Baillie in January 1823. It was finished in 1824, twelve years after he had moved in 'to occupy a very small farm house on the premises till the Muse and the Masons have made me a better'. On 27 May 1824 he wrote to a friend:

> You should come and see Abbotsford which as Augustus said of Rome (I love magnificent comparisons) I found of Brick and have left of marble. It is really a very handsome old manorial looking place both without and within, with a fine library, a Gothick hall of entrance and what not. But in truth it does not brook description any more than it is amenable to the ordinary rules of architecture – it is as Coleridge says
> > A thing to dream of not to tell.

In this extraordinary house, even long before he had put the finishing touches on its magnificence and often in the midst of noisy building operations, he entertained his friends in grand style. His custom was to rise very early and get most of his writing for the day done before breakfast. To his many guests he presented the image of a country gentleman, for whom literature was a pleasing avocation and law a nominal profession. He walked with them, rode with them, and above all took them on expeditions to see scenic splendours and historical sites. Sir Humphry Davy visited Abbotsford, and Wordsworth, and Maria Edgeworth, and the dramatist Joanna Baillie, and Washington Irving from America, with innumerable lesser folk who took Abbotsford hospitality for granted and regarded Scott and his house as public institutions to be visited. For the remarkable thing is that Scott did become a public institution, long before his authorship of the wildly popular Waverley Novels was publicly known (though it had been privately guessed by many). As early as February 1808 he was 'very much fêted and caressed . . . almost indeed to suffocation' on a visit to London. And he got his baronetcy in 1818, when he had published (anonymously) only four novels: he was known as poet, editor, antiquary, and spokesman for Scotland before the world.

Scott was an impulsive man. His whole literary career was one of impulse, largely unplanned. If a novel seemed less popular than another, if one subject was less promising, why then he would murmur one of his favourite quotations

> *If it isna weel bobbit*
> *We'll bob it again*

and start something else. And he believed that if given time he could do almost anything. Another of his favourite quotations, attributed to a Spanish monarch, was 'Time and I against any two.' A third was: 'But patience, cousin, and shuffle the cards.' This mixture of passionate opportunism and long-term confidence was

92

Bill for the sum of
£849 5s 0d made out to
Scott by James Ballantyne
on 21 June 1825

in many ways attractive. He was grateful for his popularity and for his success, but he made no great claims for himself either as poet or novelist. He would not let his own children read his poetry, considering it too trivial, and indeed his children grew up not knowing that their father was a writer. All this meant that he did not have an artist's conscience. He often wrote carelessly or mechanically. At the same time he was one of those writers who, when his imagination was really working on his material, was able, unconsciously or half-consciously, to tap a rich mine of insight into human reality in relation to the historical process. He was, one might say, a great novelist in spite of himself.

He almost crashed completely in 1813, when he avoided bankruptcy by a hairbreadth. Part of the trouble was the dealing in post-dated bills of exchange (i.e. signed promises to pay a given sum on a specified date in the future), so common at the time and so dangerous once the credit of the bill's signatory became in any way suspect. Scott used to get massive payments of this kind for his books, then discount them immediately for ready cash, using them, that is, as slightly devalued currency. 'But in these cursed times I cannot as formerly get cash for my booksellers [i.e. publisher's] bills which used to be as current as bank notes,' Scott wrote to Morritt in June 1813, asking for financial help (which he got). It was Scott's extravagance in going on buying land and also, of course, his fatal involvement in the two Ballantyne firms, both of which, especially the publishers, were now in a very rocky position, that caused the trouble. In August 1813 Scott had to ask the Duke of Buccleuch to guarantee a loan of £4,000, and indeed most of his close friends were involved in providing either credit or cash at this time. Scott's personal crisis was thus weathered, while John Ballantyne, thanks to Constable, was able to wind up without public disaster. The whole affair should have been a lesson and an awful warning to Scott, but it wasn't. It did not even trouble his conscience that he had to borrow money from his friends under what were virtually false pretences. Neither Morritt nor Buccleuch nor anyone except the Ballantynes had the remotest idea that Scott's troubles were largely the result of his financial involvement with a publishing and a printing firm. He told Morritt that he needed money to buy back his copyrights at an advantageous price and to insure his life for £4,000 to protect

94

his family if anything should happen to him. This was not honest. The £4,000 insurance policy was to cover the Duke of Buccleuch's guarantee of £4,000 and the Duke was the beneficiary.

We may blame the social ambition that forced Scott to such behaviour and wish that he had had instead rather more literary pride. Yet what drove him to behave like this was his impulsiveness, his spontaneity of feeling, his living by the needs of his imagination rather than by the sober economic realities of his life; and if this in the end destroyed him it was also bound up with his creative imagination as a novelist. There is no doubt at all that Scott loved money passionately and that his unrestrained development of Abbotsford represented great social ambition. But his love of money was not a miser's or a financier's, nor was his social ambition a matter of social climbing. He wanted to act out, with all the enlightenment of understanding and generosity of feeling that the modern world had taught him, the old traditional role of landed proprietor at the head of a social hierarchy within his domains. That is to say, he wanted to achieve by his own way of life the resolution of those tensions between tradition and progress which provide the theme of his greatest novels. It was, one can reasonably conclude, a silly ambition. But looking at Scott's life and work together, it is certainly an ambition that one can understand.

On 18 December 1825, shortly before the final crash, when Scott was hoping that it might be all right after all yet was very apprehensive, he summed up his life in the shadow of imminent disaster. He wrote in his *Journal*:

> What a life mine has been! – half educated, almost wholly neglected or left to myself, stuffing my head with most nonsensical trash, and undervalued in society for a time by most of my companions – getting forward and held a bold and clever fellow contrary to the opinion of all who thought me a mere dreamer – Broken hearted for two years – my heart handsomely pierced again – but the crack will remain till my dying day. Rich and poor four or five times, once at the verge of ruin, yet opend new sources of wealth almost overflowing – now taken in my pitch of pride, and nearly winged (unless the good news hold), because London chuses to be in an uproar, and in the tumult of bulls and bears, and a poor inoffensive lion like myself is pushd to the wall. And what is to be the end of it? God knows.

Waverley, resumed so casually in 1813, was published anonymously in 1814 and *The novelist*
its enormous success launched Scott on his unprecedentedly successful career as a novelist. It was published by the now reconciled Constable (and of course printed by James Ballantyne), on the basis of an equal division of profits between author and publisher. Unaware, or not choosing to speculate, that the publication of *Waverley* would make literary history and change his own life, Scott was off on a two-month voyage round the Scottish islands (including Shetland, where he

WAVERLEY;

OR,

'TIS SIXTY YEARS SINCE.

IN THREE VOLUMES.

Under which King, Bezonian? speak, or die!
Henry IV. Part II.

VOL. I.

EDINBURGH:

Printed by James Ballantyne and Co.

FOR ARCHIBALD CONSTABLE AND CO. EDINBURGH; AND
LONGMAN, HURST, REES, ORME, AND BROWN,
LONDON.

1814.

(Left) Title-page of the first edition of *Waverley* which bears the imprints of James Ballantyne & Co., the printers, Archibald Constable, the publisher, and Longman, Constable's London agents

(Right) Sketch by Lady Compton for Scott's copy of *The Lord of the Isles*

(Below left) 'Clausus tutus ero' stamp. The motto ('I shall be safe when closed up') may well provide the clue to Scott's insistence on anonymity as a novelist

found material he was to use later in *The Pirate*) during the very period when the fate of his book was being decided. The diary that he kept on his voyage makes no mention of *Waverley*.

A very small circle of friends was let into the secret of the authorship of the Waverley Novels, and many others guessed, but to the world in general Scott scrupulously preserved the secret, going to the point of flatly denying his authorship to friends outside the privileged circle when they asked him. 'I shall not own Waverley,' he wrote to Morritt (who was in the secret) in July 1814, 'my chief reason is that it would prevent me of the pleasure of writing again.' In his General Preface, written in 1829 after the truth was finally out, Scott simply says: 'I can render little better reason for choosing to remain anonymous, than by saying with Shylock, that such was my humour.' The reason was certainly not that he felt it shameful for a gentleman to write novels, for in his correspondence he frequently states that a gentleman can write what he likes, and for money, while in the revealing 'Introductory Epistle' to *The Fortunes of Nigel* he vigorously asserts that 'a successful author is a productive labourer, and . . . his works constitute as effectual a part of the public wealth, as that which is created by any other manufacture'. (And had not the Grand Old Man of Scottish letters of the time, Henry Mackenzie, a gentleman loved and respected, written novels?) But he seems to have had some deep-seated desire to conceal how many lives he was leading and how much his way of life was dependent on writing best-selling novels. Further, he enjoyed

mystification, as his fun and games with the anonymously published *Bridal of Triermain* clearly showed. But the real clue is perhaps provided by the motto 'Clausus tutus ero' (I shall be safe when closed up), an approximate anagram of his name in Latin and a device once borne by a much earlier Walter Scott at a tournament at Stirling, which he chose in 1809 to mark certain special copies of a historical work he had edited. The motto combines romantic associations with a suggestion of the necessity of withdrawal and privacy. Scott was a sociable man who loved good company and was always excellent company himself. But – as his *Journal* shows – there was in him too a streak of solitariness, a tendency to withhold part of himself. He seems to have felt that it would have made him *vulnerable* if he acknowledged the authorship of the Waverley Novels. In fact, he had to acknowledge the authorship in 1826 to the trustees appointed after the crash, since this was his main source of income, and in February 1827 he at last acknowledged it publicly at a Theatrical Fund dinner in Edinburgh.

Waverley is one of the great novels, arguably Scott's greatest. It contains, and finds an 'objective correlative' for, Scott's deepest insights into the conflicting claims of tradition and progress. This story of a young Englishman, his imagination stirred as Scott's had been by masses of unguided romantic reading, succumbing to the appeal of the Highland way of life on the eve of the Jacobite Rebellion of 1745, joining that Rebellion as a result, and gradually finding out the difference between the romantic and the real estimate of the Stuart cause and the nature of war, is the first historical novel in the modern sense of that term. It is not a spine-chilling evocation of Gothic horrors or an exercise in picturesque medievalizing, but a deeply imagined presentation of an historical paradox that has implications far beyond the period portrayed. In his fictional exploration of the viability of an older heroic code and its relation to rhythms of life which have in fact survived because they represent something even more fundamental to human society, Scott never – and this is true of virtually all his work – allows history alone to divide the sheep from the goats. No side contains all the heroes or all the villains; there are in Scott no historical villains. Character engages with history – men of very similar character may find themselves on opposite sides through the workings of history. And ordinary people, caught up in movements for which they have no responsibility and which they often do not fully understand, react as character and circumstance allow. It is often these ordinary people, speaking a vernacular Scots with totally convincing dramatic spontaneity, through whom Scott presents the true line of historical development.

Guy Mannering, Scott's second novel, though written much more to a conventional formula (dire prophecies, dispossession, the lost heir reappearing and finally gaining the girl *and* his inheritance) was nevertheless deeply rooted in Scottish society in the time of Scott's youth and contains some brilliant scenes of common life. It was published, in 1815, by Longman in London and Constable in Edinburgh on terms that by now Scott was in a position to dictate. Longman granted bills for £1,500 to Scott, and at the same time relieved John Ballantyne & Co. of stock to the extent of £500; and Longman sold a share of the edition to Constable. With the one exception noted below, Constable published all the subsequent Waverley Novels, and henceforth the pattern was this: Scott never parted with the copyright, but sold the right to print two-thirds of the first impression (10,000 or 12,000) for advance payment of from £2,500 to £3,000 – in bills of exchange maturing on different dates but generally discounted for cash at once by Scott. A third of the first printing was registered in the name of James Ballantyne, one-half of this belonging to Scott and the other half being divided between the two Ballantynes, James for his services as proof-reader and literary adviser, and John for his increasingly important services as agent in charge of negotiations with the publishers.

Scott's narrative poem *The Lord of the Isles* and his novel *Guy Mannering* both appeared in 1815. The relative lack of success of the former and the roaring success of the latter confirmed Scott in his career as novelist. Henceforth, with extraordinary fecundity, and sometimes by driving himself desperately because he needed the money, Scott produced an average of more than one novel a year. The victory of Waterloo, an event which stirred Scott enormously, also occurred in 1815. He made a triumphant visit to London in March and the following summer paid his first visit to the Continent primarily to see the battlefield, and met his hero

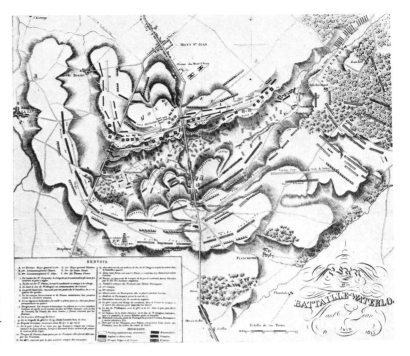

Plan of the Battle of Waterloo. 'On Wednesday last, I rode over the field of Waterloo, now for ever consecrated to immortality.' Scott to the Duke of Buccleuch, August 1815

the Duke of Wellington in Paris. The trip produced a series of letters home describing his experiences, in which autobiography is only faintly disguised. He called it *Paul's Letters to his Kinsfolk* and it was published in 1816 by Constable in Edinburgh and Murray and Longman in London. He needed the money it provided. 'I pray you push on Paul,' he wrote to John Ballantyne in October 1815. 'Taking the edition at 6000 [at] 12/– & deducting £300 already received [for travel expenses], there will be £800 & upwards to draw which will do much to clear next month.' That last phrase is significant and ominous. Scott and the Ballantynes seemed to be living perpetually at the extreme edge of their financial resources.

Scott's third novel, *The Antiquary*, appeared in May 1816. Here Scott came nearer still to his own time. The 'Advertisement' which Scott wrote as an introduction, is significant:

> The present Work completes a series of fictitious narratives, intended to illustrate the manners of Scotland at three different periods. *Waverley* embraced the age of our fathers, *Guy Mannering* that of our own youth, and *The Antiquary* refers to the last ten years of the eighteenth century.

Scott was charting a movement in the history of his own country. *The Antiquary* is almost a novel of manners, but seasoned by melodrama, humour and a strain of what Scott himself considered Wordsworthian simplicity in the treatment of the

99

sorrows of the poor. After a fairly slow start it too became a public favourite. It was Scott's own favourite among his novels.

Pushed by the need of money for his expanding Abbotsford estates, and excited by prolific ideas for more novels which danced in his head, Scott now embarked on a curious plan. Constable was in the secret as to the true author of *Waverley*: why could Scott not try another line, with another publisher, also anonymously but not to be ascribed to 'the author of Waverley'? So he invented a series called *Tales of My Landlord* collected by a fictitious schoolmaster Jedediah Cleishbotham and approached (through James Ballantyne) the Edinburgh publisher William Blackwood, agent of the London publisher John Murray. The first of the new stories was *The Black Dwarf*, which Blackwood rightly considered inferior, and showed part of the manuscript to the critic William Gifford, who confirmed his opinion. Blackwood's doubts were passed on to Scott through James Ballantyne, and Scott replied with a mighty blast:

> Dear James
> My respects to the Booksellers & I belong to the Death-head Hussars of literature who neither *take* nor *give* criticism. I know no business they had to show my work to Gifford, nor would I cancel a leaf to please all the critics of Edinburgh & London. . . . I never heard of such impudence in my life.

Scott had already shown himself touchy in the negotiations about terms. '. . . he [Murray] proposes they shall have the copyright *for ever*,' Scott wrote to John Ballantyne on 29 April. 'I will see their noses cheese first.' But eventually everything was agreed. Two novels, *The Black Dwarf* and *Old Mortality*, appeared together in four volumes in December 1816. Scott triumphantly talked of 'a 4 volume work a Romance totally different in stile and structure from the others – a new cast in short of the net which has hitherto made miraculous draughts'. John Murray and the anonymous author (who must, however, wrote Murray, be either Walter Scott or the Devil) shared the profits equally, with Murray paying the author in addition £750 for the right to sell the first edition of 6,000, with further payments for later editions; and he took several hundred pounds worth of unsaleable stock off John Ballantyne's hands. After the fourth edition Scott transferred the rights to Constable (and, as always with Scott's books published by Constable, until he later and fatally turned to Hurst Robinson & Co. instead, to Constable's London agents Longman). Scott had had qualms of conscience about deserting Constable, even though under the faint disguise of a different anonymous author. Besides, Constable offered better terms. His next novel, *Rob Roy* ('by the author of Waverley'), as well as the second series of *Tales of My Landlord* (consisting of *The Heart of Midlothian*), both published in 1818, went to Constable. John

Ballantyne got rid of more of his old stock, and Scott got in advance the usual post-dated bills.

It was in March 1817 that Scott was visited by the first of the bouts of severe internal pain which plagued him for the next three years. 'I had a most violent attack,' he wrote to Morritt, 'which broke up a small party at my house [in Castle Street, Edinburgh, where Scott always stayed when the Court of Session was sitting] and sent me to bed roaring like a bull-calf.' The trouble was eventually diagnosed as gall-stones, and after Scott had suffered interminably the then standard treatment of bleeding and blistering and had also tried dulling the pain with laudanum, what he described as his 'cramps, fits of sickness, spasms, jaundice, and all the evils that have undone me' gave way at last to calomel which, once pre-scribed and found effective, he henceforth took whenever he had an attack.

Scott tried never to let his frequent visitations of excruciating pain interfere with his writing. When he was unable to write, he dictated to his friend and factor Willie Laidlaw. He struggled through *Rob Roy* in frequent pain, and when James Ballantyne called one day and found him sitting with a clean pen and a blank sheet of paper before him, Scott replied to his remonstrance: 'Ay, ay, Jemmy, 'tis easy for you to bid me get on, but how the deuce can I make Rob Roy's wife speak with such a *curmurring* in my guts?' But the novel was finished in December, and Scott sent James the manuscript with a note:

> *With great joy*
> *I send you Roy.*
> *'Twas a tough job,*
> *But we're done with Rob.*

Rob Roy is another Scottish novel dealing with the relation between heroic violence and enlightened prudence, with merchant and brigand, city and country, Lowland and Highland, counterpointed against each other and, as always, a romantically inclined young man in between. *Old Mortality* is a more deeply imagined novel which springs from the depths of Scott's historical imagination: set in the late seventeenth century (the earliest period he had yet handled in his novels), it dealt with the struggle between fanatical Covenanters and their moral opposites the hedonistic Cavaliers, with again a man of goodwill standing in between and temporarily seduced into joining an extremist group. It is a central novel in Scott's *œuvre*, diagnosing, with brilliant relating of individual character to historical forces, one of the central crises of Scottish history and illuminating its moral and psychological meaning and its legacy to the present. It was followed by *The Heart of Midlothian*, probably the most generally admired of all Scott's novels, except for the protracted ending deliberately enlarged to make a fourth volume for which he had been paid in advance. Here we see the Covenanting tradition tamed by history into eccentricity on the one hand and on the other achieving humble personal heroism very different from the fatal violence of earlier practitioners: character and history are related in a way that gives a new dimension to the historical novel.

The third series of *Tales of My Landlord*, consisting of *The Bride of Lammermoor* and *A Legend of Montrose*, appeared in 1819. The latter is a slight work, but the former, dealing with a tragic confrontation between the old, traditional order (now dispossessed) and the new take-over class, gives great dramatic (at times even melodramatic) force to a real historical movement. Much of it was written in agony.

Scott had now written nine novels, at least four of them major works, all of them dealing with Scotland in the recent past. These were the 'Scotch novels', on which the reputation of 'the author of Waverley' was built and in which he expended the first rush of his fictional-historical imagination. Then, improvising and trying out as usual, he turned away from Scotland to a country and, more certainly, to a period which he knew less well, and in *Ivanhoe* (1820) wrote of medieval England. Though his historical imagination was working more theatrically here and the engagement of his deepest feelings was less, the novel is nevertheless a remarkable

(*Left*) Playbill for *Rob Roy Macgregor*, the play based on *Rob Roy* and the most popular of the dramatic versions of Scott's novels. It was still going strong as an annual feature when the present writer was a schoolboy in Edinburgh. (*Right*) Six stage settings by Nasmyth for *The Heart of Midlothian*

achievement, subjecting the code of medieval chivalry to the same searching moral-historical examination to which he had subjected Jacobitism, and again by means of character, though characters drawn more from the outside. It was an enormous success. He published two other novels in the same year: *The Monastery*, set in sixteenth-century Scotland and marred by a facile and unintegrated use of the supernatural, though it has magnificent scenes and well-realized characters, and *The Abbot*, its sequel, a novel full of panache and colour, with the character and dilemma of the unfortunate Mary Queen of Scots, imprisoned in Loch Leven Castle, as its moral centre.

Fourteen novels in six years – it was an extraordinary achievement, but Scott could not rest. He needed the money, the Ballantynes needed him to keep going, and Constable needed him too. ('Our most productive culture is the Author of *Waverley*,' Cadell wrote to his partner Constable in June 1822. 'Let us stick to him, let us dig on and dig on at that extraordinary quarry – and as sure as I now write to you we will do well.') It was Constable who suggested to Scott that since he had written a novel centred on Mary Queen of Scots he should write another centred on her great rival and contemporary Queen Elizabeth. The result was *Kenilworth* (1821), a novel based on an imitation ballad by W. J. Mickle about the

The actor Charles Kemble as Ivanhoe

(*Left*) Costumes for *La Marche des Costumes d'Ivanhoe* at a ball given by the Prince and Princess of Orange, 1823. (*Right*) Playbill for the dramatic version of *A Legend of Montrose*

(Left) *Fragmenta Regalia* by Sir Robert Naunton, 1642, with manuscript notes by Scott. This valuable account of Queen Elizabeth's courtiers, written in about 1630, was used by Scott to obtain background for *Kenilworth*

(Right) Rediscovery of the Scottish Regalia in the Crown Room, Edinburgh Castle, 1818

Earl of Leicester's desertion of his wife and her subsequent murder. In spite of some glaring anachronisms and a considerable amount of self-conscious 'Elizabethanizing' in the dialogue, *Kenilworth* has great vitality, and some scenes – notably the confrontation between the Earls of Sussex and Leicester before Queen Elizabeth – are truly memorable, as is the portrait of the Queen herself. Scott was also working at this time on *Lives of the Novelists* and a number of journalistic and editorial jobs, but he let nothing interfere with the flow of his fiction. He turned to Scotland again late in 1821 with *The Pirate*, a novel of late seventeenth-century Shetland in which he drew on his memories of his visit there in 1814 as well as on much historical and antiquarian reading. This was followed by *The Fortunes of Nigel* (1822), in which he drew on his wide antiquarian reading in the seventeenth century to produce a detailed and persuasive picture of Scotsmen in London in those early years of the century after James VI of Scotland had come south to become James I of England. The portrait of King James himself is one of Scott's most impressive achievements. In the same year he published *Peveril of the Peak*, dealing with religious and political conflicts in Restoration England. The plot, which has echoes of *The Fortunes of Nigel*, is laboured, and the novel shows signs of a temporarily fatigued imagination.

A public figure   But we must pause for breath (as Scott never did) to see what else Scott had been doing besides writing novels. He had managed to pay off his personal debts, Constable's generous advance for the second series of *Tales of My Landlord* having enabled him to cancel his £4,000 bond to the Duke of Buccleuch. (Constable

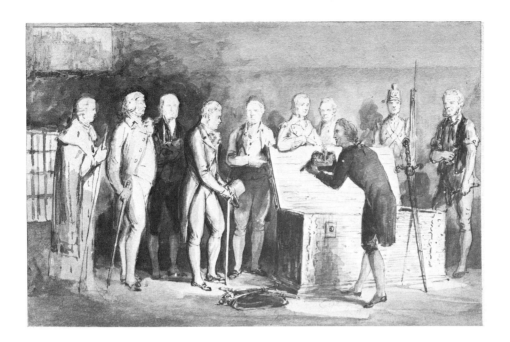

also took over, as part of this contract, the remainder of John Ballantyne's stock, and made a great loss on it.) But, building and buying land, Scott's expenses kept growing. He was more than ever an admired public figure, a lion-hunted celebrity at Abbotsford, a pillar of Edinburgh social and intellectual life at Castle Street. He was responsible for the rediscovery of the Scottish Regalia in February 1818, at a ceremony at which he showed deep emotion: when one of the officials made as though to put the newly recovered Crown of Scotland on the head of one of the young ladies standing near him, Scott cried out 'By God No!' in a voice 'between anger and despair'. The crown went back into the box – a nice symbol of Scott's relation to Scotland's violent past.

Scott's baronetcy in 1818 followed hard on the recovery of the Regalia. He had wanted it. 'Now should it consist with his Royal Highness pleasure . . . to consider me not unworthy of being distinguished by the rank above mentioned I can only say that my fortune now enables me to support it with decency and that circumstances connected with my own family & my wifes would render an honour of very great consequence to my son,' he wrote to Lord Melville in February 1818.

He kept writing to his friends that the *petit titre* (as he always called it) was of little consequence to himself, but for his son, who was making the army his profession, it would be 'useful'. He bought his son Walter's commission as a cornet in the 18th Hussars in July 1819 for £750, and spent £1,200 on his outfit. In April 1825 he bought him a captaincy for £1,500. Scott was devoted to his children, and extremely proud of his son Walter. He liked to think of himself as the founder of a

The Scottish Sword of State, part of the Scottish Regalia

(*Above left*) Sir Walter Scott as baronet. (*Above right*) Sophia Scott, 'a most attached and dutiful daughter who never in her life gave me five minutes' vexation'. (*Below*) Sketch and description of Scott's arms

Arms used by Scott to decorate the entrance hall, Abbotsford

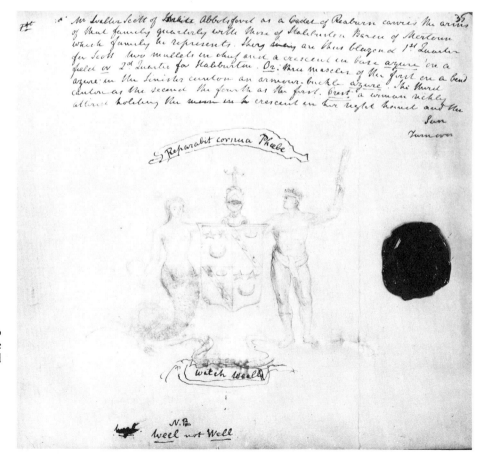

(*Left*) John Gibson Lockhart. 'He is a young man of uncommon talents, highly accomplished, a beautiful poet and fine draughtsman, and what is better of a most honourable and gentlemanly disposition.' Scott to Lady Abercorn. (*Right*) James Hogg, 'The Ettrick Shepherd'

dynasty, with his son succeeding. Fortunately he could not know that both his sons would die childless and comparatively young, and that the title would die with the second Sir Walter.

In 1818 Scott first met John Gibson Lockhart, a young literary advocate of strong Tory views who wrote for the newly founded *Blackwood's Edinburgh Magazine*, a more sensational Tory periodical than *The Quarterly*. In its first issue of October 1817, *Blackwood's* had published a shocking satire on Edinburgh notables, in mock-biblical prose, entitled 'The Chaldee Manuscript'. This was the joint work of Lockhart, James Hogg, 'The Ettrick Shepherd' whom Scott had consistently helped, and John Wilson, who wrote under the pen-name of Christopher North. 'It fell on Edinburgh like a thunderbolt,' Scott's future son-in-law later wrote, and gave great scandal to the Whigs. In the same issue of *Maga* (as *Blackwood's* came to be popularly called) there was a violent and unscrupulous attack on Coleridge in the guise of a review of *Biographia Literaria* and an equally violent attack on the morals of Leigh Hunt in the first of two notorious articles on 'The Cockney School of Poetry'.

Scott was no lover of this kind of journalism, but he liked Lockhart's wit and respected his classical scholarship and wide reading in modern languages. The result was a friendship between the older and younger man, accompanied by several warnings from the former to the latter to keep away from anonymous

abusive journalism. (How right he was. It was anonymous abusive journalism that led to the duel between John Scott – no relation of Walter's – and Lockhart's close friend Jonathan Christie, which proved fatal to John Scott.) Lockhart married Scott's daughter Sophia in April 1820, and the couple lived at Chiefswood (on the now extensive Abbotsford estates) until Lockhart left for London to take up the editorship of *The Quarterly* in 1825. Lockhart lived in close association with Scott in the last twelve years of Scott's life, and this gives a vividness and an immediacy to his biography of his father-in-law, which remains, with Scott's letters, the major source of our knowledge of Scott in spite of what we now know to be some deliberate distortions, evasions and even inventions.

Scott was in London in July 1821 for the coronation of George IV, and returned with plans for further elaborate work on Abbotsford, including the library and the drawing-room, which eventually made it into the house we now know. This meant more money, of course, and as usual it was to be paid for by advances on novels not yet written. Robert Cadell, Constable's partner, replied to Lockhart's query as to why Scott produced so much so promptly: 'December 1819 saw the completion of *Ivanhoe* – March 20 of *The Monastery*, *The Abbot* in September and *Kenilworth* in the January following. . . . Scott still depended on the appearance of each new novel for the bills it was to produce.' The death of Charlotte's brother Charles in India seemed likely to improve the Scott finances: Scott wrote to his friends that Charles had left over £30,000, interest on which was to go to the widow for her lifetime after which the capital was to go to Scott's children in equal portions. But Scott grossly over-estimated what the amount

ATION OF HIS MOST GRACIOUS MAJESTY, KING GEORGE THE FOURTH.
iew from Westminster Hall to the Abbey. Showing the appearance of the surrounding Buildings &c &c &c on the 19th of July 1821.

(*Above*) Coronation of King George IV, 19 July 1821, which Scott attended. (*Left*) Pass for
Sir Walter Scott to the Coronation signed by Lord Melville, the second viscount

eventually turned out to be, and in any case Charles's widow outlived both Scott
and all his children. But it is interesting evidence of the way that Scott was becoming
more and more obsessed by money that he should have written cheerfully to several
of his friends crowing about the expected £30,000.

Yet he was a happy man. Summing up his life in a letter to an old friend in 1821
he wrote: 'I have had an affectionate and promising family – many friends – few
unfriends and I think no enemies – and more of fame and fortune than mere
literature ever procured for a man before. I dwell among my own people and have
many whose happiness is dependent on me and which I study to the best of my
power. I trust my temper which you know is by nature good and easy has not been
spoiled by flattery or prosperity and therefore I have escaped entirely that irritability
of disposition which I think is planted like the slave in the poet's chariot to prevent
his enjoying his triumph.' Scott had a capacity for happiness. He loved being
Laird of Abbotsford; he loved both the pleasures of the family circle (he was a
genuinely good father) and the social excitement of entertaining guests; he loved –
really loved – his dogs; he loved being a 'kenspeckle' (conspicuous) figure in
Edinburgh; and, in spite of so often teetering on the edge of financial disaster, he
loved negotiating his contracts with publishers and the golden showers they
produced. He seems to have had no qualms about accepting bills for large sums for
work which he had not yet started. 'Time and I against any two.'

Of course, he had implicit faith in Constable's financial soundness. He thought his children's future was secured by his brother-in-law's bequest. And then young Walter was handsomely settled in the military profession. All the young man needed was an attractive, sympathetic, loving and very wealthy wife. And his father found one for him. Meditating on Walter's future in March 1824, he remembered or seemed to remember a very mild flirtation the young man and Miss Jane Jobson had indulged in some years before. He wrote to his son, suggesting 'in a mystical sort of way' that Jane Jobson, 'the pretty heiress of Lochore', might be a suitable match. But only if Walter, having renewed his acquaintance with her, found her really attractive and the attraction was mutual. In a second letter on the subject he wrote: 'The sight of the beautiful woods and valley of Lochore may perhaps have influenced my judgement but I conversed with her [Jane] a good deal and when her shyness wore off found her pleasant and totally unaffected.' So Walter and Jane came together again, were indeed mutually attracted, and, in spite of the initial resistance of Jane's mother, were married early in 1825. (Scott settled the entire estate of Abbotsford upon the young couple, to be enjoyed after his death, subject only to the condition that he could raise a mortgage of £10,000 on it if it proved necessary – which it later did.) Scott was at a peak of happiness. It was not only that he saw young Walter settled in life, with an heiress as wife of whom he wrote to a friend: 'There is gold in her garters for her fortune in land and property is £50,000 and possibilities.' But he became at once genuinely devoted to Jane to whom he wrote some of the most charming and happy letters he ever penned. Indeed, the letters he wrote in the spring of 1825 show Scott brimming over with content. One cannot help being moved by the affectionate, high-spirited, playful letters he wrote to his 'darling Jane' when she was in Ireland where her husband was stationed. 'Good night darling and take care of yourself,' he ends one letter. There is nothing else like this in the whole body of Scott's correspondence.

More novels   And still the novels came. After the laboured *Peveril of the Peak* in 1822, and the interruption of work that year during the visit of George IV, he went on to produce one of his greatest successes, *Quentin Durward*, published in 1823. Here for the first time he ventured outside the British Isles, to fifteenth-century France, whose atmosphere of decaying chivalry – a historical situation just right for Scott's imagination – he was able to render with remarkable persuasiveness in spite of relatively little detailed knowledge of the period and no first-hand knowledge of the topography. The portrait of Louis XI is one of Scott's triumphs. The book was enthusiastically received in France and was important in extending Scott's reputation throughout the Continent. The next year saw the publication of *St Ronan's Well*, an extraordinary mixture of contemporary novel of manners and Gothic melodrama in which Scott seems to have mistrusted his own imagination and so botched what might have been one of his most original works: this has never

THE BALANCE OF PUBLIC FAVOR.

Balance of Public Favour, 1827: Thomas Moore outweighing Scott and all the volumes of Napoleon. In fact Scott remained the favourite

been a popular novel of Scott's, though it possesses its own kind of interest. He had recently been elected Chairman of the Edinburgh Oil Gas Company (which ended up by making a loss, and Scott had to pay up his guaranteed amount in December 1827). In 1824 he was active in helping to found a new secondary school in Edinburgh, the Edinburgh Academy.

In the spring of 1824 Scott wrote to James Ballantyne: 'I never liked St Ronan's – this I think better of.' 'This' was *Redgauntlet*, published that year, in which he triumphantly returned to his first theme, the fate of Jacobitism in the modern world. The two young men of the novel, Darsie Latimer and Alan Fairford, are aspects of himself; Mr Fairford is his father; and Green Mantle is his never-forgotten first love. But these facts are only important as an indication of how deeply engaged Scott's true self was in this remarkable novel, in which the history and fate of modern Scotland are explored in a manner both illuminating and moving. The great scene of the dissolution of the last belated attempt at a Jacobite rebellion, 'not with a bang but a whimper', is one of the finest things Scott ever wrote and an important key to the meaning of all his novels about Scotland.

The year 1825 saw the publication of his two 'Tales of the Crusaders', *The Betrothed* and *The Talisman*, the former of which neither Scott nor James Ballantyne thought much of, nor indeed has anybody else, but the latter, which contrives both to give the excitement of chivalric activity and to expose it as swagger and violence to be contrasted unfavourably with the art and science of the Saracens, has always been among the most popular of the Waverley Novels. In 1825, too, he started work on his massive biography of Napoleon (about whom he had radically changed the violent and contemptuous opinion of his younger days), which was to

Napoleon's bee clasps owned by Scott

(*Above left*) Maria Edgeworth. In the concluding chapter of *Waverley* Scott expressed his wish 'in some distant degree to emulate the admirable Irish portraits drawn by Miss Edgeworth'

(*Above right*) Anne Scott. Anne never married, but remained at home to look after her widowed father

(*Left*) *The Great Unknown lately discovered in Ireland*, 1825. According to Lockhart, when Scott, on his visit to Dublin in 1825, entered a street, 'the shopkeepers and their wives stood bowing and courtseying all the way down; while the mob and boys huzza'd as at the chariot wheels of a conqueror'

cost him more research and more labour than any other of his works and the financial proceeds of which were to be so important to him after the crash. (It was published in nine volumes in 1827.) And in July 1825, together with Lockhart and his unmarried daughter Anne, he made an excursion to Ireland, to see young Walter and his adored daughter-in-law and to visit the admired Maria Edgeworth whose novels, he always maintained, had originally inspired him to try to do for Scotland what she had done for Ireland. He was fêted in Dublin, in the manner to which he had by now become accustomed.

Lockhart's departure for London with his wife and small son in November left Scott lonely and feeling old. In other respects also late 1825 was an ominous period. There had been great speculative fever in London. 'They who had accumulated great masses of wealth,' wrote Lockhart, 'dissatisfied with the usual rates of interest under a conscientious government really protective of property, had embarked in the most perilous and fantastic schemes for piling visionary Pelions

The crash

Gala Day at Abbotsford. Scott was a great believer in local celebrations and encouraged various kinds of beanfeasts among the Abbotsford tenantry

Bubbles for 1825 or *Fortunes made by Steam*, 1824. This gives some indication of the atmosphere that produced the crash involving Scott, Constable and Ballantyne

upon the real Ossa of their money-bags; and unscrupulous dreamers, who had all to gain and nothing to lose, found it easy to borrow, from cash-encumbered neighbours, the means of pushing adventures of their own devising, more extravagant than had been heard of since the days of the South Sea and Mississippi bubbles.' Robinson, of Hurst, Robinson & Co., the firm which had succeeded Longman as Constable's London agent and on which therefore both Constable and Scott and James Ballantyne (John had died in 1821) all depended financially, had speculated ruinously in hops and there were rumours that the firm could not meet their obligations. An anxious Constable, as usual heavily in debt to the future, worried by the fate of those numerous bills of exchange and accommodation bills (bills granted by X to Y for services Y was to perform for Z, who would then eventually pay Y so that X could get his money back, and often simultaneously granted by Y to X for the same amount) hurried to London to see what could be done. Scott, in Edinburgh for the autumn session, working hard and unusually slowly at his *Napoleon*, listened nervously to rumours and hoped for the best. The simple fact was that the whole vast edifice of credit backed by bills on which Constable, Scott and Ballantyne had been living was about to crumble.

It was in this mood of anxiety that Scott began his *Journal* on 20 November 1825. He records his impressions of Ireland, complains about the number of strangers who descend on Abbotsford, and registers his 'purpose to practise economies'. On 14 December he records his anxiety 'about the money-market in London'. He decides to borrow £10,000 on the Abbotsford estate, which his son's marriage contract allowed. He reckons up his debts and his resources. Four days later the worst seems to have happened. 'Cadell has received letters from London which all but positively announce the failure of Hurst and Robinson so that Constable & Co. must follow and I must go with poor James Ballantyne for company. I suppose it

Scott was a passionate lover of dogs. Maida (*left*), a Scottish deerhound, is probably the best known. (*Right*) Ginger, by Landseer

Dear Walter

I am truly sorry to write what will give you pain to read but an event has taken place which in a worldly point of view has carried away a most serious proportion of my worldly goods. This is the sudden and most unexpected Bankruptcy of Constable and Company here and their Agents and correspondents Hurst and Robinson in London both within these three weeks accounted the largest houses in London & Edinburgh & thus were safe. They had in their hands many engagements of mine for which I have wrought hard and will now not only not get a farthing but be obliged to pay back the cash I have received. How their affairs will turn out is uncertain but I look to be a great loser and may perhaps be so further than I at present calculate. It is hard at my time of life. But as every body here is inclined to give me time I must hope that. I will neither be a poor knight[?]. I am not afraid of any body losing a penny and I trust with good management I may even save my land though it will be by reducing my scale of expense very much. But I would give up much rather than part with Abbotsford and as James[?] [...]

The first page of Scott's letter to his son Walter announcing the crash

will involve my all. But if they leave me £500, I can still make it £1,000 or £1,200 a year . . . I have been rash in anticipating funds to buy land, but then I made from £5,000 to £10,000 a year, and land was my temptation.' He wonders how he could bear to go on living in a place where he was once wealthy and honoured, but gets some satisfaction from recalling that his children are provided for. He will have to put down his dogs. 'I find my dogs' feet on my knees – I hear them whining and seeking me everywhere – this is nonsense, but it is what they would do could they know how things are – poor Will Laidlaw!' But later that evening Cadell arrived to tell him that Hurst Robinson had withstood the storm and all might yet be well. On Christmas Eve he set off for Abbotsford in confident mood. But on 26 December he felt sick and ill, with a violent pain in his right kidney, and he had to take calomel. On 16 January, back in Edinburgh now, he wrote: 'Hurst and Robinson have suffered a bill of £1,000 to come back upon Constable, which I suppose infers the ruin of both houses. We will soon see.' On 17 January James Ballantyne & Co. stopped payment, after Archibald Constable & Co. – Constable having failed in his desperate attempts to raise credit in London – had done likewise. Scott was a ruined man. On 22 January he wrote in his *Journal*:

I feel neither dishonoured nor broken down by the bad – miserably bad news I have received. I have walked my last on the domains I have planted – sate the last time in the halls I have built. But death would have taken them from me if misfortune had spared them. My poor people whom I loved so well! There is just another dye to turn up against me in this run of ill-luck – *i.e.*, if I should break my magic wand in the fall from this elephant, and lose my popularity with my fortune. Then *Woodstock* [his latest novel] and *Boney* may both go to the paper-maker, and I may take to smoking cigars and drinking grog, and turn devotee, and intoxicate the brain another way. In prospect of absolute ruin, I wonder if they would let me leave the Court of Session. I would like, methinks, to go abroad,
        'And lay my bones far from the *Tweed*'.
But I find my eye moistening, and that will not do. I will not yield without a fight for it. . . .

Cockburn recorded memorably how Scott's ruin affected Edinburgh:

The opening of the year 1826 will ever be sad to those who remember the thunderbolt which then fell on Edinburgh in the utterly unexpected bankruptcy of Scott, implying the ruin of Constable the bookseller, and of Ballantyne the printer. If an earthquake had swallowed half the town, it would not have produced greater astonishment, sorrow, and dismay. Ballantyne and Constable were merchants, and their fall, had it reached no further, might have been lamented merely as the casualty of commerce. But Sir Walter! The idea that his practical sense had so far left him as to have permitted him to dabble in trade, had never crossed our imagination. How humbled we felt when we saw him – the pride of us all, dashed from his honourable and lofty station, and all the fruits of his well-worked talents gone. He had not then even a political enemy. There was not one of those whom his thoughtlessness had so sorely provoked, who would not have given every spare farthing he possessed to retrieve Sir Walter.

Well do I remember Scott's first appearance after this calamity was divulged, when he walked into Court one day in January 1826. There was no affectation, and no reality, of *facing it*; no look of indifference or defiance; but the manly and modest air of a gentleman conscious of some folly, but of perfect rectitude, and of most heroic and honourable resolutions. It was on that very day, I believe, that he said a very fine thing. Some of his friends offered him, or rather proposed to offer him, enough money, as was supposed, to enable him to arrange with his creditors. He paused for a moment; and then, recollecting his powers, said proudly – 'No! this right hand shall work it all off!'

Schedule of bills forming the sum of £10,505 13s 7d, all drawn by Constable & Co. mostly on James Ballantyne & Co., prepared after the crash. The firm's total obligations came to £256,000. It went bankrupt and paid 2s 9d in the pound

Sir Walter Scott, by Sir David Wilkie

When you consider that after the 31st. of December next, only four Volumes of the annotated Edition of the Novels will have to appear, that no gain can arise from the Poetical Works until the sales of them shall have liquidated a considerable debt, which stands against that Series, that the Miscellanies in prose, are in a similar situation, that the publication of the Works of the deceased can not go on without the incurrence of heavy charges for editing and superintending; and lastly, that there is a considerable new debt which must be met in some way, we trust the present communication may be regarded by you as not unworthy to be submitted at some early date, to a General Meeting of the Creditors.

It is obvious that we ventured on a heavy responsibility which may eventually bring personal embarrassment on ourselves. To do this we have felt it our duty; and we shall be consoled whatever may be the result, with the reflection that we have done our utmost towards executing the purposes which our venerated Parent had in view, when he drew up the disposition that has caused us to come before you.

We have the honour to be

Your obedient humble Servants,

Signed { *Walter Scott*
       Charles Scott
       J. G. Lockhart.

To
Messrs Gibson, Jollie, & Monypenny,
Trustees for Sir Walter Scotts Creditors.

Closing paragraph of the copy of the minutes of the meeting of the creditors of Messrs. James Ballantyne & Co. and of the late Sir Walter Scott, Bart, and Mr James Ballantyne, 29 October 1832

Scott's own reaction, and his state of mind in the few years of declining health left to him, is movingly told in his *Journal*, a remarkable work from which only lack of space forbids lavish quotation. He bore himself with a resigned and positively proud stoicism, though indeed he had not behaved quite as honourably as he and Cockburn believed. For example, Abbotsford was settled on young Walter and therefore was not, as Ballantyne and his creditors supposed, available as a source of cash or credit. And there were tradesmen, owed money by Scott, who could not afford to wait indefinitely for their money: Scott never seemed aware of this. But he was determined to pay everything off with his pen, and set himself to spend the rest of his life to write steadily to that end. His major creditors were considerate: they agreed to set up a private trust into which Scott would pay the proceeds of his writings in order eventually to clear his debts. These amounted to £116,838 11s 3d, of which £20,066 19s 9d were his private debts; £12,615 6s 7d due by James Ballantyne & Co. or for which both partners were liable, bonds contracted on behalf of Archibald Constable & Co. for which Scott was liable, to the amount of £9,129 9s 0d; and £75,026 15s 11d in the form of discounted bills in the hands of third parties. In addition there was the mortgage of £10,000 secured over the estate of Abbotsford. By the time of his death eleven shillings in the pound had been acknowledged by the trustees towards clearing off the debts of 1826, but Scott,

The last years

119

whose style of living did not diminish to the extent he at first determined, incurred further personal debts. He continued to enjoy his salary as Sheriff and as Clerk of Session. He sold the house in Castle Street, and lived in Abbotsford, the trustees agreeing to let him keep the furniture and library. When he had to be in Edinburgh for his Court duties he stayed in rented lodgings.

Woodstock, a novel of seventeenth-century English history, well plotted and told with spirit, was finished in March 1826 and bears no obvious signs of the strain under which it was written. It was offered to Longman, and the trust made over £6,000 from it. Scott then turned again to his dogged labours on *Napoleon*, for which Longman now agreed to pay a total of 10,500 guineas. His decision was certainly paying off. Meanwhile, Scott continued to receive visitors, especially old friends, and there were still some happy days – and nights – at Abbotsford.

A rush of patriotic Scottish feeling in March 1826, when the Government proposed to legislate to prevent the Scottish banks from issuing their own bank-notes, led him to attack the proposal fiercely in his *Letters of Malachi Malagrowther*, which much annoyed his Government friends. Scott was getting more and more agitated at the prospect of parliamentary reform, and saw the maintaining of traditional Scottish institutions as one way of preventing it. His Toryism hardened unpleasantly in his last years, and he made a sad fool of himself at an election meeting in Jedburgh in May 1831 when, confused and sick, he intervened on behalf of the Tory candidate and aroused the wrath of the populace.

Stornoway one pound note of 1823. Scott's three *Letters of Malachi Malagrowther* were directed against the Government's proposal to prevent banks other than the Bank of England from issuing their own notes as money and thus against the issuance of local notes in Scotland. They had their effect: Scottish banks still issue their own notes

A 'Malachi Malagrowther' note of 1846 which shows the long-standing effect of Scott's three *Letters*

John Hugh Lockhart and Walter Scott
Lockhart. For the former, Scott wrote
Tales of a Grandfather

For his health was going. Chilblains, rheumatism, worsening lameness, worried him increasingly. But he kept on writing. In 1827 he published *Chronicles of the Canongate*, a volume of three short stories one of which *The Two Drovers*, is particularly fine. The second series of *Chronicles of the Canongate* was *The Fair Maid of Perth*, published in 1828, a novel of medieval Scotland which shows no sign of falling off. And, in addition to a variety of miscellaneous works, he produced between 1828 and 1831 four series of *Tales of a Grandfather*, Scottish history recounted for his little grandson John Hugh Lockhart; *Anne of Geierstein* (1829) a somewhat laboured novel, but done with energy; *Count Robert of Paris* and *Castle Dangerous*, both published in 1832, which do show a distinct falling off. And well they might. On 15 February 1830 Scott had the first of several cerebral haemorrhages which left him temporarily speechless and paralysed. He recovered, more or less, and ignored his doctor's advice by insisting on continuing to write. One of the projects that occupied him in these final years was what he called the *opus magnum*, planned as a fully annotated edition of all the Waverley Novels.

It was Scott's increasingly embattled Toryism that finally estranged him from his old friend James Ballantyne, who had survived bankruptcy to find employment as manager and later (with his brother Alexander) owner of the printing firm he and Scott had founded. Ballantyne wrote an article supporting parliamentary reform; Scott summoned him to Abbotsford to explain himself, and after words between the two James left in anger. Scott's friends had to restrain him from entering the fray with a violent anti-reform pamphlet.

Meanwhile, the Government – ironically, the Whig administration of Lord Grey – realizing that Scott was ill, offered to put the frigate *Barham* at his disposal for a cruise in the winter of 1831-2. Scott, urged by his doctors, accepted. Wordsworth came to Abbotsford from the Lake District for a farewell visit on 21 September, and on the twenty-third Scott, with his daughter Anne and Lockhart, set off for London. Scott felt weak and, as he recorded in the *Journal*, mentally confused. Yet in London he continued to receive visitors and to lead a social life. Finally, on 29 October, he sailed on the *Barham* from Portsmouth. They visited Malta, where they spent some time, then spent some time in Naples. Scott suffered further minor strokes and sometimes was very confused. But he continued to behave as though he were still capable of writing novels, and there were periods of mental clarity and social liveliness. He wrote letters, and continued with his *Journal*. His last entry records his starting from Naples on 16 April 1832.

Abbotsford, 1830. A comment on Scott's tenacity and determination in the face of trouble and illness

I've set open the Flood Gates and if they are simple enough to place themselves in its way, they do it at their own peril.

NOBLE LORDS OPPOSING THE TORRENT OF REFORM.   "Let your means be adequate to the end Proposed"

Noble Lords opposing the Torrent of Reform, October 1831. Scott was strongly against the Reform Bill, but in one of his last really lucid moments, in Rome in May 1832, he said to Edward Cheney that he was no enemy of reform. 'If the machine does not work well, it must be mended – but it should be by the best workmen ye have'

Pro-Reform crowds in the streets cheering a speaker, December 1831. 'I regard your gabble no more than the geese on the green': Scott to a Pro-Reform crowd in Jedburgh, in March 1831

From this time on Scott could think of nothing but getting back to Scotland. He would talk of nothing but Scotland, and compared every scene in north Italy to which his attention was drawn to some Scottish scene. He was sinking steadily both mentally and physically. They got him back to Abbotsford on 11 July: Lockhart's account of the journey home is one of the most moving things in biographical literature. His old friend and factor Willie Laidlaw was waiting for him at the porch when they carried him in, bewildered, until his eye fell on Willie and he exclaimed: 'Ha! Willie Laidlaw! O man, how often have I thought of

(*Above*) View of the Eildon Hills from Ladshope Moor, looking towards Melrose. Scott must have seen this identical view on his last journey home

(*Right*) The bridge at Torwoodlee. 'But as we descended the vale of the Gala he began to gaze about him and by degrees it was obvious that he was recognizing the features of that familiar landscape. Presently he murmured a name or two – "Gala Water, surely – Buckholm – Torwoodlee."' (Lockhart)

William Laidlaw, one of Scott's dearest
friends

you!' Once at home, he rallied briefly, and then declined painfully until his death
on 21 September.

It is significant that Scott died in the year of the Reform Bill. His historical
imagination worked magnificently up to that point, but could not see beyond. He
belonged both to the Romantic Revival and to the Scottish Enlightenment, and
the blend of the two is like nothing else in our literature. In many ways he was a
rationalist. Fascinated though he was by superstition, he was not in the least
superstitious himself, and once cheerfully slept in an inn room where a corpse lay
on the other bed. 'Superstition is very picturesque, and I make it at times stand
me in great stead,' he once remarked, 'but I never allow it to interfere with
interest or convenience.' As for religion, he detested the zeal of the Covenanters
(he once called them 'a set of cruel and bloody bigots') and wrote contemptuously
of the Church as a profession to Lockhart when the latter suggested it as a profession
for Charles. He believed that enthusiasm in religion was perhaps good for the
lower classes, 'for it is a guard against gross & scandalous vice', but among the
upper classes 'can do nothing but evil disuniting families setting children in
opposition to parents and teaching as I think a new way of going to the Devil for
Gods sake'. He believed – or rather hoped – in immortality and he believed in a
beneficent Creator. That is about as far as his religion went, except that he liked
these beliefs seasoned with tradition.

As for his character, the testimony of his contemporaries is unanimous. He was
loved as well as admired. With our hindsight we can see and criticize his self-
deceptions, his mercenary streak, his impetuosity. We can now see too, quite
clearly, his shocking artistic negligence, yet at the same time we can see how this is

Scott's favourite view of the Tweed from the dining-room of Abbotsford. In his last days he was taken to lie in this room so that he could see his beloved Tweed. This photograph was taken from the roof, as the trees Scott planted now obscure the view of the Tweed from the dining-room windows

bound up with the almost effortless flow of his deeply perceptive historical imagination. And we can see also how deeply his response to history was involved in the peculiar poise of Scottish history in his own day, caught up both in enlightened progress and in nationalistic antiquarianism, in the plans for the New Town of Edinburgh as well as with fascination with the Old. He spoke uniquely for Scotland between the 'Forty-Five and the Reform Bill. He judged the past by the present and the present by the past, but he lacked altogether the Wellsian feeling for the future. That lack was understandable and indeed inevitable. It was part of his negligent genius. And in the last analysis genius he was, without qualification.

Scott's death mask

(*Below*) Scott's funeral procession. '. . . when the coffin was taken from the hearse, and again laid on the shoulders of the afflicted serving-men, one deep sob burst from a thousand lips.' (Lockhart)

Scott's Tomb at Dryburgh Abbey, where he had decided at an early age that he wanted to be buried

Buchan, John *Sir Walter Scott* (1932)

Clark, Arthur M. *Sir Walter Scott. The Formative Years* (1969)

Cockburn, Henry *Memorials of His Time* (1856)

Corson, James A. *A Bibliography of Sir Walter Scott* (1943)

Gillies, R. P. *Recollections of Sir Walter Scott* (1837)

Grierson, H. J. C. *Sir Walter Scott, Bart* (1938)
   The Letters of Sir Walter Scott (12 vols, 1932–7)

Hogg, James *The Domestic Manners and Private Life of Sir Walter Scott* (1834)

Johnson, Edgar *Walter Scott: The Great Unknown* (2 vols, 1970)

Lang, Andrew *Life of Sir Walter Scott* (1906)

Lockhart, J. G. *Memoirs of the Life of Sir Walter Scott* (7 vols, 1837–8)

Muir, Edwin *Scott and Scotland* (1936)

Partington, Wilfrid (ed.) *The Private Letter-Books of Sir Walter Scott* (1930)
   Sir Walter's Post-Bag (1931)

Pearson, Hesketh *Walter Scott His Life and Personality* (1954)

Quayle, Eric *The Ruin of Sir Walter Scott* (1968)

Tait, J. G. *The Journal of Sir Walter Scott* (3 vols, 1939–46)

1771 [or perhaps 1770] 15 August: Walter Scott born at Edinburgh

1773 An illness leaves him permanently lame in his right leg. Convalescences at Sandy-Knowe, at the home of his grandfather.

1779 Begins attendance at the High School, Edinburgh.

1783 Stays at the Border town of Kelso where he attends the local grammar school.
November: enters Edinburgh University.

1785 Illness. Convalescence at Kelso at the home of an uncle sympathetic to his literary interests.
Begins five years' apprenticeship in the legal profession to his father.

1792 11 July: admitted to the Bar. Summer spent in Border country.

1793 Summer in the Perthshire Highlands.

1796 Anonymous publication of *The Chase, and William and Helen*, translations by Scott from Gottfried August Bürger.

1797 24 December: marries Charlotte Carpenter. They take up residence in Edinburgh.

1799 Publication of Scott's translation of Goethe's *Goetz von Berlichingen*.
Obtains appointment as Sheriff-depute of Selkirkshire.

1802 Publication of *The Minstrelsy of the Scottish Border* vols I and II.

1804 Rents small country-house, Ashestiel, on the Tweed.

1805 Publication of *The Lay of the Last Minstrel*.
Partnership agreement with the printer James Ballantyne.

1806 Obtains the reversion of the office of Clerk of Session but does not receive emoluments until 1812.

1808 Publication of *Marmion* and Scott's edition of Dryden.

1809 Scott responsible for founding the firm of John Ballantyne & Co., booksellers and publishers.

1810 Publication of *The Lady of the Lake* by Ballantyne & Co.

1811 The lease of Ashestiel expires and Scott buys the property of Abbotsford on which he lavishes money in enlargements and improvements until his crash.

1813 Financial crisis. John Ballantyne wound up, rescued by the publisher Constable.

1814 Anonymous publication of *Waverley*. Scott by now a prominent public figure.

1815 Battle of Waterloo.
Scott visits London and the Continent.
The publication of *Guy Mannering* and *The Lord of the Isles*. With the success of the former following that of *Waverley* Scott embarks on an extraordinarily productive period as a novelist.

1818 Accepts baronetcy.

1821 Interrupts a busy social and literary life to visit London for the Coronation of George IV.

1822 Supervises George IV's visit to Scotland.

1825 Visits Ireland.
Begins biography of Napoleon.
20 November: begins *Journal*.

1826 Bankruptcy on the failure of the publishing companies of Constable, Hurst and Robinson and of the printing firm of James Ballantyne.
Death of his wife.
In his last years the will to clear his debts spurs Scott to dogged literary output.

1831 Health failing. Mediterranean cruise on the frigate *Barham* with his daughter Anne and Lockhart.

1832 Returns to Scotland.
21 September: death at Abbotsford.

NOTES ON THE PICTURES

Frontispiece: SIR WALTER SCOTT reading the Proclamation of Mary Queen of Scots previous to her marriage to Darnley; oil by William Allan, 1832. *National Portrait Gallery, London.* Scott was fascinated by the unfortunate Queen and more than once said that his heart and his head gave contradictory verdicts on her

5 A TRUE HISTORY of Several Honourable Families of the Right Honourable Name of Scot by Capt. Walter Scot. Edinburgh, 1688; title-page and fly-leaf with a manuscript verse by Scott. *By kind permission of Mrs Maxwell-Scott. Photo Eileen Tweedy.* This 'rude but enthusiastic clan poetry was in all likelihood about the first book of verses that fell into the poet's hand'. (Lockhart: *Memoirs of the Life of Sir Walter Scott, Bart*)

6 THE YARROW. *Photo Alan Daiches*

7 THE EILDON HILLS. *Photo The Scottish Tourist Board*

GALASHIELS looking South to Gala Hill. *Photo Alan Daiches*

8 DRYHOPE TOWER, ST MARY'S LAKE; engraving by J. Heath after J. C. Schetky. From Scott: *The Lay of the Last Minstrel,* 1810. *British Museum, Department of Prints and Drawings*

THE EILDON HILLS; aquatint by Merigot after Girten, 1801. *Edinburgh Public Libraries*

9 'BEARDIE' WALTER SCOTT, Scott's great-grandfather; oil by William Aikmann. *By kind permission of Mrs Maxwell-Scott. Photo National Galleries of Scotland*

10 WALTER SCOTT, Scott's father; oil by ?Robert Harvie, *c.* 1758. *By kind permission of Mrs Maxwell-Scott. Photo National Galleries of Scotland*

ANNE RUTHERFORD, Scott's mother, as an old woman; oil by John Watson Gordon. *By kind permission of Mrs Maxwell-Scott. Photo National Galleries of Scotland*

11 THE ABBOT OF UNREASON; engraving by George Cruikshank for Scott: *The*

Abbot. From C. Rogers: *The Centenary Garland,* 1871. *British Museum.* 'The Roman Catholic Church . . . connived, upon special occasions, at the frolics of the rude vulgar, who assumed the privilege of making some Lord of the revels, who, under the name of the Abbot of Unreason . . . profaned the holy places.' (Scott: note to Chapter IV of *The Abbot*)

12 THE HOLY BIBLE given to Scott by his mother, 1 January 1819; title-page and fly-leaf with a manuscript genealogy of the Scott family and a dedication to Scott by his mother, under which Scott wrote: 'This Bible was . . . alas! the very last gift which I was to receive from that venerable parent.' *By kind permission of Mrs Maxwell-Scott. Photo Eileen Tweedy*

13 VIEW OF EDINBURGH showing the Old and New Towns; aquatint by John Wells after R. Barker. From R. Barker: *Panoramic View of the City of Edinburgh,* 1790. *British Museum, Map Room*

THE HIGH STREET, EDINBURGH, before the removal of the Luckenbooths; pen and wash drawing by David Allan, 1793. *Edinburgh Public Libraries*

15 COLLEGE WYND, EDINBURGH; tinted pencil drawing by James Drummond, 1856. For A. Kerr: *Old Edinburgh,* 1879. *Scottish National Portrait Gallery, Edinburgh.*

16 PLAN OF EDINBURGH OLD TOWN; engraving from J. and H. S. Storer: *Views in Edinburgh and its Vicinity,* vol. I, 1820. *British Museum*

PLAN OF EDINBURGH NEW TOWN; engraving from J. and H. S. Storer: *Views in Edinburgh and its Vicinity,* vol. I, 1820. *British Museum*

GEORGE SQUARE, Edinburgh; water-colour by P. Paton *National Gallery of Scotland, Edinburgh, Department of Prints and Drawings*

18 OAKWOOD TOWER-BOHILL-ETRICK WATER, Selkirkshire; wash drawing by James Skene, 1804. *Edinburgh Public Libraries*

19 ROBERT SCOTT of Sandyknowe, Scott's grandfather; oil by ?Robert Harvie. *By kind permission of Mrs Maxwell-Scott. Photo National Galleries of Scotland*

THE VICTORY obtain'd over the Rebels at Culloden, by the Duke of Cumberland. Tandem Triumphans (The Pretender's Motto), translated by the Duke of Cumberland with the point of his sword; engraving, 1746. *British Museum, Department of Prints and Drawings*

21 MANUSCRIPT of *Marmion,* 1808. *Trustees of the National Library of Scotland, Edinburgh.* Adv. MS. 19.1.16

23 SANDIE KNOW OR SMAILHOLM TOWER; wash drawing by James Skene, 1830. *Edinburgh Public Libraries*

24 DE ONTHOOFDING van de Rebellige Lords op Groot Tower Hill; engraving, 1746. *British Museum, Department of Prints and Drawings*

25 WALTER SCOTT aged six; miniature painted at Bath, 1777. *By kind permission of Mrs Maxwell-Scott. Photo National Galleries of Scotland*

26 EDINBURGH. From the base of the Calton Hill; lithograph by T. M. Baynes, 1823

27 HIGH SCHOOL, Edinburgh; engraving by J. and H. S. Storer. From J. and H. S.

Storer: *Views in Edinburgh and its Vicinity*, vol. II, 1819. *British Museum*

28 DR ALEXANDER ADAM (detail); oil by Henry Raeburn, *c.* 1808. *Scottish National Portrait Gallery, Edinburgh*

29 JOHN GRAHAM of Claverhouse, Viscount Dundee; miniature. *Scottish National Portrait Gallery, Edinburgh*

SWORD OF MONTROSE presented to Scott by John Ballantyne. *By kind permission of Mrs Maxwell-Scott. Photo Eileen Tweedy*

30 THE BLIND OSSIAN singing and accompanying himself on the harp; watercolour sketch by Alexander Runciman for the ceiling decorations at Penicuik House. *National Gallery of Scotland, Edinburgh, Department of Prints and Drawings*

31 THE REIVER'S WEDDING, or, the *Ballad of Muckle Mou'd Meg*; watercolour by Charles Kirkpatrick Sharpe. *By kind permission of Mrs Maxwell-Scott. Photo National Galleries of Scotland*

32 JEAN DE LA VALETTE; lithograph by Mlle Formentin. From Le Vicomte L.-F. de Villeneuve-Bargemont: *Monumens des Grands Maîtres de l'Ordre de Saint-Jean de Jérusalem*, 1829. *Victoria and Albert Museum, London*

33 VIEW OF KELSO BRIDGE AND ABBEY; engraving by F. Jukes after C. Catton, 1793. *British Museum, Map Room*

34 THE INSIDE VIEW OF MELROSE ABBEY; engraving by F. Jukes after C. Catton, 1798. *British Museum, Map Room*

35 BIRD'S EYE VIEW OF EDINBURGH from the south (detail); engraving by James Gordon after P. de Wit, 1647. *Edinburgh Public Libraries*

36 PRINCE CHARLIE'S QUAICH owned by Scott. *By kind permission of Mrs Maxwell-Scott. Photo Eileen Tweedy*

37 A CHART, WHEREIN ARE MARK'D ALL THE DIFFERENT ROUTS OF P. EDWARD IN GREAT BRITAIN, and the Marches of his Army and the English; engraving, 1746. *British Museum, Department of Prints and Drawings*

39 ROBERT BURNS AND WALTER SCOTT in James Sibbald's Bookshop, Edinburgh, 1786; oil by William Borthwick Johnstone. *Edinburgh Booksellers' Society.*

40 GLEN OF THE TROSSACHS; engraving by C. Turner after H. W. Williams. *British Museum, Map Room*

43 ROB ROY'S DIRK AND PURSE owned by Scott. *By kind permission of Mrs Maxwell-Scott. Photo Eileen Tweedy*

44 AN ETYMOLOGICAL DICTIONARY OF THE SCOTTISH LANGUAGE by John Jamieson, 1808; page with a manuscript note by Scott relating to *Marmion*, 1808. *By kind permission of Mrs Maxwell-Scott. Photo Eileen Tweedy*

47 SCOTT'S MANUSCRIPT COPY of Hume's lectures on Scots Law, *c.* 1791. *By kind permission of Mrs Maxwell-Scott. Photo Eileen Tweedy*

48 THE DOUGLAS RING which Scott found in the Hermitage Castle, Liddesdale. *By kind permission of Mrs Maxwell-Scott. Photo Eileen Tweedy*

HERMITAGE CASTLE, Liddesdale; pen drawing. *By kind permission of Mrs Maxwell-Scott. Photo Eileen Tweedy*

49 ROBERT SHORTREED; silhouette. *Scottish National Portrait Gallery, Edinburgh*

MIST IN LIDDESDALE. *Photo Alan Daiches*

50 JOHN THE LITTLE SCOTT; a song collected by Scott in Liddesdale, *c.* 1795, and rejected for *Minstrelsy of the Scottish Border, 1802. By kind permission of Mrs Maxwell-Scott. Photo Eileen Tweedy*

THE BIRTHPLACE OF JAMES HOGG, 'The Ettrick Shepherd', Ettrick; engraving by Daniel Wilson after D.O. Hill. *Edinburgh Public Libraries*

51 WALTER SCOTT in the ruins of the Hermitage; oil by Henry Raeburn, 1808. *Duke of Buccleuch and Queensberry, K.T., G.C.V.O. Photo Courtauld Institute of Art*

53 GEDICHTE by Gottfried August Bürger. Gottingen, 1796; title-page. *By kind permission of Mrs Maxwell-Scott. Photo Eileen Tweedy*

GOETZ OF BERLICHINGEN, with the iron hand: a Tragedy. Translated from the German of Goethe by Walter Scott, Esq., Advocate, Edinburgh. London, 1799; title-page. *British Museum*

55 GLAMIS CASTLE; watercolour by ?Thomas Cocking; *National Gallery of Scotland, Edinburgh, Department of Prints and Drawings*

56 LETTER FROM SCOTT TO CHARLOTTE CARPENTER, 22 November 1797, prior to their marriage. *Trustees of the National Library of Scotland, Edinburgh, MS. 138, no. 16, f. 3*

57 CHARLOTTE CARPENTER, Lady Scott; miniature, *c.* 1797. *By kind permission of Mrs Maxwell-Scott. Photo Eileen Tweedy*

CHARLOTTE CARPENTER, Lady Scott (detail); oil by James Saxon, *c.* 1805. *By kind permission of Mrs Maxwell-Scott. Photo National Galleries of Scotland*

59 HENRY DUNDAS, first Viscount Melville; oil by Thomas Lawrence, 1810. *National Portrait Gallery, London.* 'He, at least his nephew, was my early patron, and he gave me countenance and assistance when I had but few friends.' (Scott to George Ellis, 3 March 1806)

THOMAS MUIR ESQ., THE YOUNGER, of Huntershill, tried by Lord Braxfield for urging reforms; engraving by John Kay, 1793

61 WALTER SCOTT, second baronet; oil by William Allan, *c.* 1822. *By kind permission of Mrs Maxwell-Scott. Photo National Galleries of Scotland*

64 BOTHWELL BRIDGE; engraving by W.H. Lizars after A. Nasmyth, 1821. From *Sixteen Engravings from Real Scenes Supposed to be Described in the Novels and Tales of the Author of Waverley, 1821. British Museum, Department of Prints and Drawings*

65 WALTER SCOTT in the uniform of the Edinburgh Light Dragoons; miniature given to Charlotte Carpenter on her engagement to Scott, 1797. *By kind permission of Mrs Maxwell-Scott. Photo National Galleries of Scotland*

JOANNA BAILLIE; watercolour by William Newton. *British Museum, Department of Prints and Drawings*

66 SCOTT'S COTTAGE, LASSWADE; pencil and brown wash, 1798. *National Gallery of Scotland, Edinburgh, Department of Prints and Drawings.*

39 NORTH CASTLE STREET, EDINBURGH. *Photo Alan Daiches*

67 CHARLES MACKAY as Bailie Nicol Jarvie in *Rob Roy*; oil by William Allan, 1825. *By kind permission of Mrs Maxwell-Scott. Photo National Galleries of Scotland.*

68 GEORGE IV AT HOLYROOD HOUSE presented with the Palace keys by the Duke of Hamilton; oil by David Wilkie, c. 1822. *Scottish National Portrait Gallery, Edinburgh*

THE ENGLISH-IRISH-HIGHLANDER; woodcut from an English broadside, 1822. *British Museum, Department of Prints and Drawings*

69 THE DEPUTY RANGER'S HOUSE (The Royal Lodge), Windsor; watercolour by Paul Sandby, c. 1800. *Windsor Royal Library*, no. 14634. 'Went down to Windsor, or rather, to the Royal Lodge in the Forest, which . . . seems to be no bad specimen of a royal retirement.' (Scott: *Journal*, 20 October 1826)

71 ILLUSTRATION to *The Lay of the Last Minstrel;* pen and wash drawing by William Allan. *National Gallery of Scotland, Edinburgh, Department of Prints and Drawings*

72 ASHESTIEL; watercolour sketch for the frontispiece of *Marmion* by J. M. W. Turner, c. 1808. *Fitzwilliam Museum, Cambridge*

ASHESTIEL from across the Tweed. *Photo Alan Daiches*

73 THE DUCHESS OF BUCCLEUCH (detail); watercolour by T. Heaphy, 1805. *The Duke of Buccleuch and Queensbury, K.T., G.C.V.O. Photo National Galleries of Scotland*

JAMES BALLANTYNE; pencil and brown wash drawing by John Ballantyne. *Scottish National Portrait Gallery, Edinburgh*

PAUL'S WORK, Edinburgh; pencil and brown wash drawing by John Ballantyne, 1810. *Scottish National Portrait Gallery, Edinburgh*

75 ARCHIBALD CONSTABLE (detail); oil by Andrew Geddes, c. 1800. *Scottish National Portrait Gallery, Edinburgh.*

JOHN BALLANTYNE (detail); oil. *Scottish National Portrait Gallery, Edinburgh*

77 A HEALTH TO LORD MELVILLE; a song written by Scott to celebrate Melville's acquittal in June 1806. This copy was included by Scott in a letter to Robert Dundas, 1806. *Trustees of the National Library of Scotland, Edinburgh.* MS 933, f. 52r.

79 WALTER SCOTT as Clerk of the Court; pencil drawing on the fly-leaf of a book by Mark Napier, 1829. *Trustees of the National Library of Scotland, Edinburgh.* R.Y.IV.E. 21

80 RING GIVEN TO SCOTT ON THE DEATH OF LORD BYRON, 1824. *By kind permission of Mrs Maxwell-Scott. Photo Eileen Tweedy*

81 BYRON in the Highlands; lithograph by Currier and Ives. *Newstead Abbey Collections. Nottingham Public Libraries, Local History Library*

82 LOCH KATRINE from the west end; engraving by Joseph Swan after J. Fleming. *Edinburgh Public Libraries*

83 ABBOTSFORD seen through the gateway; watercolour by William Allan, 1832. *National Gallery of Scotland, Edinburgh, Department of Prints and Drawings*

AIR COMPRESSION BELL in the drawing-room at Abbotsford. *By kind permission of Mrs Maxwell-Scott. Photo Eileen Tweedy*

84 WILLIAM ERSKINE, Lord Kinedder; watercolour. *Scottish National Portrait Gallery, Edinburgh*

85 MANUSCRIPT of *Waverley*, 1805–14. *Trustees of the National Library of Scotland, Edinburgh.* Adv. MS. 1.1.0, f. 31v.

86 MELROSE; watercolour by J. M. W. Turner, *c.* 1819. For Robert Cadell's edition of Scott: *Poetical Works*, 1830. *National Gallery of Scotland, Edinburgh, Department of Prints and Drawings*

87 CARTLEY HOLE (nicknamed Clarty Hole), as it was in 1812; watercolour. *By kind permission of Mrs Maxwell-Scott. Photo Eileen Tweedy*

ABBOTSFORD; pencil drawing by J. W. Ewbank. *National Gallery of Scotland, Edinburgh, Department of Prints and Drawings*

ABBOTSFORD; watercolour by Anne Nasmyth. *National Gallery of Scotland, Edinburgh, Department of Prints and Drawings.* 'I assure you Don Quixote might be pardoned if he took Abbotsford for an absolute Castle.' (Scott to Richard Heber, 12 November 1823)

88 A HILL RUN with the Duke of Buccleuch's hounds; oil by Francis Grant. *The Duke of Buccleuch and Queensberry*, K.T., G.C.V.O. *Photo National Galleries of Scotland*

THE RHYMER'S GLEN; pencil drawing by J. W. Ewbank. *National Gallery of Scotland, Edinburgh, Department of Prints and Drawings*

89 WALTER SCOTT; bust by Francis Chantrey, 1828. *Scottish National Portrait Gallery, Edinburgh*

ABBOTSFORD from the northern bank of the Tweed, with the Scott family picnicking in the foreground; oil on a japanned metal tray by J. M. W. Turner, begun 1831. *Indianapolis Museum of Art. Gift in memory of Evan F. Lilly with the hope that this will bring beauty and inspiration into the lives of others*

90 THE LIBRARY, ABBOTSFORD; proof engraving after William Allan for J. G. Lockhart: *Memoirs of the Life of Sir Walter Scott, Bart*, 1837. *By kind permission of Mrs Maxwell-Scott. Photo Eileen Tweedy*

GOTHIC HALL, PALL MALL. Catalogue of a Splendid Collection of Military Antiquities. London, 1819; title-page. *By kind permission of Mrs Maxwell-Scott. Photo Eileen Tweedy*

ENTRANCE HALL, ABBOTSFORD. *By kind permission of Mrs Maxwell-Scott. Photo Eileen Tweedy*

91 ABBOTSFORD. *Photo Alan Daiches*

93 WALTER SCOTT; oil sketch by Edwin Landseer, 1833. *The Duke of Buccleuch and Queensberry*, K.T., G.C.V.O. *Photo National Galleries of Scotland*

94 A BILL for the sum of £849 5s 0d sterling, made out to Scott by James Ballantyne on 21 June 1825. *Trustees of the National Library of Scotland, Edinburgh.* Adv. MS. 15.1.20, p. 12, no. 34

96 WAVERLEY; or, *'Tis Sixty Years Since*. Edinburgh, 1814; title-page of the first edition. *British Museum*

'CLAUSUS TUTUS ERO'; library stamp at Abbotsford. *By kind permission of Mrs Maxwell-Scott. Photo Eileen Tweedy*

97 VIEW IN THE HEBRIDES; pencil drawing by Lady Compton in Scott's copy of *The Lord of the Isles*, 1815. *By kind permission of Mrs Maxwell-Scott. Photo Eileen Tweedy*

99 PLAN de la Bataille de Waterloo ou Mont-Saint-Jean, 18 Juin 1815; engraving. *British Museum, Department of Prints and Drawings*

102 ROB ROY MACGREGOR, or, *Auld Lang Syne*; playbill for the Theatre Royal, Covent Garden, 12 March 1818. *Victoria and Albert Museum, London, Enthoven Collection*

SIX STAGE SETTINGS for *The Heart of Midlothian*, to be performed at the Theatre, Edinburgh; pen drawings by Alexander Nasmyth, 1819–20. *National Gallery of Scotland, Edinburgh, Department of Prints and Drawings*

103 MR C. KEMBLE as Ivanhoe; engraving. *Victoria and Albert Museum, London, Print Room*

COSTUMES for La Marche des Costumes d'Ivanhoe, au bal donné par L.L. AA.R. et J. le Prince et la Princesse d'Orange, 1823; lithograph by F.L. *Trustees of the National Library of Scotland, Edinburgh*

MONTROSE; or *The Children of the Mist*; playbill for the Theatre Royal, Covent Garden, 14 February 1822. *Victoria and Albert Museum, London, Enthoven Collection*

104 FRAGMENTA REGALIA by Sir Robert Naunton, 1642, with manuscript notes by Scott on overslips. *By kind permission of Mrs Maxwell-Scott. Photo Eileen Tweedy*

105 DISCOVERY OF THE SCOTTISH REGALIA in the Crown Room, Edinburgh Castle, 4 February 1818; pencil and brown wash. *National Gallery of Scotland, Edinburgh, Department of Prints and Drawings*

SWORD OF STATE, part of the Scottish Regalia; pencil drawing by ?Andrew Geddes; c. 1818. *By kind permission of Mrs Maxwell-Scott. Photo Eileen Tweedy*

106 CEILING BOSSES IN THE ENTRANCE HALL, ABBOTSFORD, showing the arms of Scott's ancestors. Scott could not trace a complete heraldic line of eight shields for his mother's family and the last three shields are painted over with clouds to show how time has hidden them. *By kind permission of Mrs Maxwell-Scott. Photo Eileen Tweedy*

WALTER SCOTT after receiving his baronetcy; oil by Thomas Lawrence, 1820–26. *Reproduced by gracious permission of Her Majesty the Queen*

SOPHIA SCOTT (detail); watercolour by William Nicholson, 1818. *By kind permission of Mrs Maxwell-Scott. Photo National Galleries of Scotland*

SKETCH FOR THE ARMS OF SIR WALTER SCOTT with manuscript notes on the heraldry; pencil, c. 1821. *Trustees of the National Library of Scotland, Edinburgh.* MS. 1566, f. 35r.

107 JOHN GIBSON LOCKHART (detail); oil. *Scottish National Portrait Gallery, Edinburgh.*

JAMES HOGG, 'The Ettrick Shepherd'; oil by William Nicholson. *Scottish National Portrait Gallery, Edinburgh*

108 SIR WALTER SCOTT'S PASS for the Coronation of George IV, 1821, signed by Lord Melville, the second viscount. *By kind permission of Mrs Maxwell-Scott. Photo Eileen Tweedy*

109 CORONATION of His Most Gracious Majesty, King George the Fourth. An

exact representation of the procession from Westminster Hall to the Abbey, showing the appearance of the surrounding buildings &c. &c. on the 19th July 1821; engraving, 1822. *Guildhall Library, London*

111 THE BALANCE OF PUBLIC FAVOUR. Thomas Moore and his *Epicurean* outweighing Scott and *Napoleon*; lithograph, 1827. *British Museum, Department of Prints and Drawings*

NAPOLEON'S GOLD BEE CLASPS owned by Scott. *By kind permission of Mrs Maxwell-Scott. Photo Eileen Tweedy*

112 MARIA EDGEWORTH; engraving after Adam Buck, 1787. From Caw: Scott Gallery, 1903. *British Museum*

ANNE SCOTT (detail); watercolour by William Nicholson, 1818. *By kind permission of Mrs Maxwell-Scott. Photo National Galleries of Scotland*

THE GREAT UNKNOWN lately discovered in Ireland; engraving by R.C., 1825. *British Museum, Department of Prints and Drawings.*

113 GALA DAY at Abbotsford; oil sketch by William Allan, 1827. *Scottish National Portrait Gallery, Edinburgh*

BUBBLES FOR 1825 – or – *Fortunes made by steam*; engraving, 1824. *British Museum, Department of Prints and Drawings*

114 MAIDA; stone mounting-block at Abbotsford by John Smith, c. 1824. *By kind permission of Mrs Maxwell-Scott. Photo Eileen Tweedy*

GINGER; watercolour by Edwin Landseer. *By kind permission of Mrs Maxwell-Scott. Photo National Galleries of Scotland*

115 LETTER from Scott to his son, Walter, 26 June 1826, telling him of the crash. *Trustees of the National Library of Scotland, Edinburgh.* MS 139, no. 58, f. 1

117 SCHEDULE OF BILLS forming the sum of £10,505 13s 7d. From the *Volume Containing Claims, Inventories, etc. Relating to the Bankruptcy of Constable & Co. and Robert Cadell Respectively, 1826. Trustees of the National Library of Scotland, Edinburgh.* MS. 802, f. 27v.

118 WALTER SCOTT; oil by David Wilkie, 1824. *By kind permission of the Faculty of Advocates, Edinburgh. Photo National Galleries of Scotland*

119 MANUSCRIPT COPY of the Minutes of the Meeting of the Creditors of Messrs James Ballantyne & Co. and of the Late Sir Walter Scott, Bart and Mr James Ballantyne, held at Edinburgh, and within the Royal Exchange Coffee House, the 29th day of October 1832. *Trustees of the National Library of Scotland, Edinburgh.* MS. 1554, f. 63r.

120 STORNOWAY ONE POUND BANK NOTE dated 21 January 1823. *The Institute of Bankers Collection of Paper Money, London*

A MALACHI MALAGROWTHER ONE POUND BANK NOTE dated 10 March 1846. *The Institute of Bankers Collection of Paper Money, London*

121 JOHN HUGH LOCKHART AND WALTER SCOTT LOCKHART; pencil and watercolour drawing by Daniel Maclise, 1827. *By kind permission of Mrs Maxwell-Scott. Photo National Galleries of Scotland*

122 ABBOTSFORD; lithograph from *The Looking Glass*, 1 June 1831. *Victoria and Albert Museum, London, Print Room*

139

140

INDEX

Page numbers in italics indicate illustrations